Contents

Introduction

As part of a government initiative, more children than ever are attending pre-school establishments, and a pre-school curriculum has been developed that must be available in all establishments. An inspection process has been installed and all settings are expected to deliver the full curriculum, which is based upon a series of early learning goals. This, in turn, has resulted in changes in course regulations and occupational standards.

This is not a theoretical book about play and learning experiences, although each chapter has a short general introduction. It is a highly practical guide to all activities that should be available to young children from 0 to 7:11 years and is laid out in an accessible format.

The chapter on working professionally should help you to evaluate your practice and to ensure that you are always aware of equal opportunities and new educational initiatives. It will also aid you should you need to present your work in a portfolio. Charts are included as appendices, linking the activities with the National Curriculum and with National Vocational Qualifications (NVQ) Occupational Standards in Early Years Care and Education.

Activities for the 2- to 7:11-year-olds are explored first, as we regard these as the core of the book. Babies and toddlers have their own sections, and are dealt with slightly differently.

Tables are included in each chapter to show at a glance the amount and type of space required for each experience and the type of play the activity should promote. Supervision by an adult is necessary for all play experiences, but some will gain more from closer adult involvement and interest than others.

The book includes lists showing what materials are essential, and suggests additional equipment. Always buy the best quality equipment that can be afforded. When using items reflecting other cultures, you must be aware of any cultural or religious significance attached to them, and use them in an appropriate way.

The value of each activity to the child is outlined, ensuring that a broad curriculum will be offered and that all areas of development are encouraged and promoted. This is especially useful if you have a child who appears to be delayed in one area of development, as you will be able to see very quickly how to help. Another child may be gifted in one or more areas of development and may need additional stimulation and opportunities for extended exploration.

There is an emphasis on good practice, highlighting factors that are important in your planning, presentation and evaluation of the experiences you offer children. When working with children, life is not always predictable, and from time to time plans may go awry. Do not be despondent, learn from your mistakes, and try again.

All activities, equipment, toys, games, and books must reflect our diverse society, and you need to be aware of children who may have particular special needs. Whatever you are presenting should be seen as part of the everyday environment, and not as something exotic and different. The sections on equal opportunities will help you to focus on these matters.

The environment in which you work needs to be a safe and pleasant place. The paragraphs pointing out safety factors should help you to be aware of any potential hazards, either in the room or in the equipment chosen.

At the end of each chapter a useful resource list has been added and there is a larger general resource list at the end of the book.

About the Authors

The authors come from a background of nursery teaching and health visiting, and have worked together for many years training students to work with young children. They have written nine books encompassing most areas of the child-care and education curriculum.

Acknowledgements

The authors would like to thank Teresa O'Dea, Cynthia Isaac and Anna Mennell for their time and generosity; colleagues and students in the Child and Social Care Programme Area at City and Islington College for their support and encouragement; and Christopher Satterthwaite for the photographs used to illustrate the text, which were taken at the Margaret McMillan Centre.

We are particularly grateful to Judith Enenmoh for the examples of a curriculum plan (pages 124–128) and a detailed activity plan (pages 130–132) and to Carly Tyler for the example of a routine plan (pages 134–139).

Part 1

Working Professionally

When you provide activities for children, whether this provision is in the family setting or in pre-schools and schools, it is important to understand why you are doing so, and appreciate the benefits to children's development and learning. A professional childcare and education worker will be aware of the latest educational initiatives, current and past research and the importance of providing activities within the framework of the early years curriculum.

Working in a professional manner involves careful planning and preparation of all activities, thoughtful and flexible implementation, and a thorough evaluation of each activity that in turn contributes to future planning.

1 *Working Professionally*

$\mathbf{M}$uch of the work that is carried out with young children in your placement is in the form of activities, most of which are provided and structured by the staff team. Some can be unstructured and spontaneous and allow the children to use their imagination and develop close peer relationships.

The value of activities for young children

The activities that you provide should promote the children's all-round development and learning, and be both well planned and well prepared. You will need to take time to evaluate the outcomes of the activities. They should be age-appropriate and reflect our diverse multiracial society. All the children should have equal access to all the activities, regardless of language fluency, racial origin, gender, culture, class or disability.

Consultation and planning is necessary with other members of the team, so that early learning goals are achieved or the requirements of the National Curriculum are fulfilled. Your observations of children, both individually and in a group, will also play a major part in determining the particular activity you might plan to do.

Planning your activities includes making sure that:

■ you have sufficient materials for the whole class to take part, if they should so wish
■ there is time to carry out the activity to a satisfactory conclusion
■ there is sufficient suitable space available
■ there is another adult free to help you, if the activity requires it.

Using this book should help you to plan and prepare activities efficiently, and to be aware of the development and learning outcomes for the children for each of the activities you choose to do. Equal opportunities and safety must always be in the forefront of your mind in any work you plan with the children.

When you have completed an activity you need to take time to think carefully and objectively about how the children responded, what they learnt, and what areas of development were promoted and extended. Even a disaster can be a positive learning experience for you and will improve the quality of your future practice.

Make sure you participate in offering the full range of activities. Practice makes perfect! For example, if you avoid music sessions as a student, it will be more difficult for you to provide them once you are qualified.

Early learning goals

In the last few years there have been more children experiencing pre-school education, and the government is implementing a national childcare policy in which it is investing large sums of money. Any establishment wishing to receive funding from the government has to provide an appropriate curriculum based on current good practice developed in consultation with early years professionals. It is expected that by providing this curriculum, children will reach the level of learning required by the time they leave the reception class.

The areas of learning include:

- language and literacy
- mathematical development
- creative development
- personal, social and emotional development
- knowledge and understanding of the world
- physical development.

This is known as the Foundation Stage.

Baseline assessment

This was introduced into schools in September 1998. Children will be assessed during their first seven weeks of primary education. The assessment must cover language and literacy, mathematics, and personal and social development. The assessment schemes will vary from school to school. The aim of baseline assessment is to allow the teacher to find out about each child's knowledge and abilities, in order to plan effectively for each child's learning needs. It will also enable the school to measure and monitor children's progress from when they enter school so as to check levels of achievement.

Activity

Within your group, obtain the assessment schemes used in your placement.
1 Note how they vary.
2 What areas of learning are included in the scheme?
3 Discuss how parents have been prepared for the assessment, and how they have reacted to the scheme.

The National Curriculum

As you start working with children of 5 years and over in an educational setting, you will be involved in the delivery of the National Curriculum. This is laid down by the Department of Education and Employment, and must be followed by each child. The National Curriculum is divided into attainment targets that are statements of the outcomes to be achieved at specific stages in a child's schooling. These stages are known as Key Stages. Key Stage 1 is for 5–7 year-olds. At each Key Stage children are required to do a series of Standard Assessment Tasks (SATS). Practical activities are an excellent way of delivering parts of the National Curriculum, and we have included some charts on pages 142–144 that will help you to plan your activities with the National Curriculum goals in mind.

In a school, everything you take part in will have an educational and developmental outcome. You will need to keep in mind the development of the whole group as well as individuals, and to be aware of the standards that the children need to attain. If you are carrying out an activity such as cooking, you need to be conversant with the mathematical and scientific concepts that should be explored, and the language which is being used and understood.

If you use the charts on pages 142–144 as part of your preparation, you will find them helpful as you identify concepts and plan ahead, and encourage and extend the learning that is taking place. They should be useful also in evaluating the activity afterwards.

Evaluating performance

A professional person becomes adept at evaluating his or her own performance and practice. When working with children from 2 to 7:11 years this includes planning all the activities you undertake with the children, and evaluating the success or otherwise of the play experience. To help you do this, you might like to use the evaluation chart on page 145.

Monitoring for equal opportunities

You will become more and more aware, during your course, of the rights of all children and their families to equality of opportunity, and the importance of anti-discriminatory practice. The chart for monitoring of equal opportunities on page 146 will help you ensure that the activities you are providing give equal opportunities to all the children, and you may find it useful to use this from time to time to monitor your perception and sensitivity in this area.

National Vocational Qualifications

Many of you using this book may be involved in acquiring National Vocational Qualifications (NVQs) in Early Years Care and Education, either at Level 2 or or Level 3. There are mandatory and optional units at each level. NVQs are designed mainly for people already working with children, who wish to be assessed on their performance and practice against the prescribed standards by an NVQ assessor. Although there are no formal examinations, candidates are expected to demonstrate underpinning knowledge and understanding of childcare and education. We have linked the activities in this book with the relevant units of NVQs. See the charts on pages 147–149.

Part 2

Activities for Young Children

2 to 7:11 Years

The chapters in Part 2 look at a range of activities that are frequently enjoyed by children and that offer opportunities to promote their development and learning. After an introduction to the activity, we have looked at the time and space needed to implement the activity successfully. We have listed the essential materials needed and suggested additional equipment that might extend the play.

We point out in these chapters the value of each activity to the children's development and learning, underpinned by equality of opportunity and the need for safety. Each chapter outlines good practice and offers a resources list.

2 *Natural and Malleable Materials*

Natural materials are readily available and very familiar. Water, sand, clay, mud and wood, unlike most materials provided for young children, cost nothing, or very little. Because of their familiarity, it is easy to involve children in planning their own experiences with natural materials, and asking them to decide what tools and equipment they wish to use.

Malleable materials include clay and mud and any other material that can be moulded in the same way, such as dough and plasticine. These materials can be used for modelling as well as providing tactile sensory experiences.

Water

This is the most familiar of all the natural materials. Nearly all babies grow to love their bath time, and the enjoyment of water is carried through to adulthood; swimming is a favourite leisure activity. Children find playing with water enjoyable and therapeutic. Water is an indestructible material and children can bang and splash without harm. It is as usual to find the quiet child at the water tray, playing contentedly on his/her own as it is to find a noisy group using the equipment provided and finding out about floating and sinking. Playing with water links home and school. Children learn that water comes in many forms: as snow, rain, steam, and ice, and is essential for life.

AMOUNT OF SPACE		TYPE OF SPACE	
Whole area		Outside	■
Half area		Inside	■
Quarter area		Hard surface	■
Small area	■	Carpeted	
		Table space	
TYPE OF PLAY		**INVOLVEMENT OF ADULT**	
Solitary	■	Essential	
Parallel	■	Enriching	■
Small group	■	Not always necessary	■
Large group		Can be intrusive	

ESSENTIAL MATERIALS

Water of a tepid temperature

Containers: a water tray; if in the child's home, a sink, basin, baby bath or the bath could be used

Towel

Protective clothing for children: aprons, sleeves, shower caps

Floor mop

SUGGESTED ADDITIONAL EQUIPMENT

Colour: vegetable dyes, non-toxic powder paint

Detergent for bubbles; pipes and tubing

Dolls and dolls' clothes

Sieves, plastic cartons with holes in

Objects that float or sink: golf balls, stones, erasers, paper etc.

Graded vessels

Decorators' brushes and small buckets for water painting

Waterwheels and hoses

Boats made in class

Props for imaginative play, such as dinosaurs or toy fish

Leaves, pieces of bark, shells, sponges, seaweed

Good Practice

- Water must be clean and of a pleasant temperature. It should be changed twice a day, and the temperature topped up. The equipment and tray need to be cleaned and washed regularly. The children could help with these tasks.
- Children must be protected. Keep the floor as dry as possible so that children do not slip and fall. Very young children must be carefully supervised and never left alone, as babies can drown in one or two inches of water. Fully cover clothing so that children do not get wet and chilled. Dry hands after play. Ensure children with eczema spend only a short time at the water tray and their hands and arms should be very carefully dried afterwards.
- Numbers must be limited to suit the size of the tray. This can easily be done by limiting the number of aprons available.
- The tray should be sited away from the quiet area, but within easy access of an adult, and near a water supply.
- All equipment should be in good condition and should be visible and accessible to the children. Labelling and classifying will aid the learning experience.
- The chosen activity should be age-appropriate. Children should be involved in choosing it and encouraged to experiment. There should be a good range of equipment to give the children the widest variety of experiences.
- Never fill the tray with tools and equipment, but make sure that there is enough for each child to use without too much turn-taking.

VALUE TO AREAS OF DEVELOPMENT AND LEARNING

Physical
Lifting and pouring water develops arm muscles and hand-eye coordination. Picking up and placing equipment exercises manipulative skills and promotes correct use of tools.

Social and moral
Children learn to take turns and share equipment, which leads to cooperation in other areas. They have to learn and accept certain safety rules. Playing in a small group is a social activity. Shy children can become involved at their own pace.

Emotional
Children find water play therapeutic, enjoyable, relaxing and calming. No goals have to be achieved as there is no end product.

Intellectual
Using different equipment, many mathematical, scientific and technological concepts may be explored. Concentration is promoted. It may lead to imaginary play. Decisions have to be made by the children.

Language
Children will communicate needs and will become familiar with correct terminology, such as volume and density.

Aesthetic and spiritual
Watching the sun play on water and looking at reflections, colours, bubbles and rainbows promotes an appreciation of the wonders of the natural world.

Sensory
The properties of the material are explored through the varied sensory experiences: feeling the water, its movement and temperature; seeing the reflections, colours, bubbles and movements of the water and objects on or in it; and listening to the sounds of the water.

Activity
List as many examples as you can of mathematical concepts that water play promotes, giving the equipment you would use to encourage each concept.

Sand

As sand is not found indoors in the home, although some children have sand pits in their gardens, it is generally less familiar to children than water. Almost without exception, infant school classes, nurseries and playgroups will provide sand trays, and most will give the experience of wet and dry sand to the children.

Dry sand is relaxing and therapeutic to play with. A great deal can be learnt with the use of various tools. It is not suitable for very young children, unless closely supervised, as they tend to throw it around and get it in their eyes and hair as well as eat it.

Wet sand is suitable for all age groups. It can be used as a modelling material, and can be combined with blocks and cars and other small world toys to stimulate the imagination. It will lend itself to many mathematical, scientific and technological experiments.

AMOUNT OF SPACE		TYPE OF SPACE	
Whole area		Outside	■
Half area		Inside	■
Quarter area		Hard surface	■
Small area	■	Carpeted	
		Table space	
TYPE OF PLAY		**INVOLVEMENT OF ADULT**	
Solitary	■	Essential	
Parallel	■	Enriching	■
Small group	■	Not always necessary	■
Large group	■	Can be intrusive	■

ESSENTIAL MATERIALS

Washed or silver sand, available from builders' merchants – check that no chemicals have been used

Two containers, one for wet sand and one for dry sand

Broom, dust pan and brush

SUGGESTED ADDITIONAL MATERIALS

Dry sand: similar tools and containers to those used for water play, with the addition of rakes, sand combs, scoops, etc.

Shower cap to protect long or curly hair

Wet sand: buckets and spades, moulds, small world toys, vehicles with wooden blocks for ramps and building, rakes, shells, etc.

Flat trays for pattern making and early printing

Good Practice

- Sand must be kept clean. Outside, sand must be totally covered and the cover secured when not being used. If swept up from the floor, the sand must be washed thoroughly and all grit and dirt removed before being put back in the sand tray. To do this, place sand in container, pour on water to cover, and the dirt will rise to the surface.
- It is sensible to site the indoor sand trays away from carpeted areas, so that spilt sand can be swept up easily. Adults and children should have ease of access to the sand.
- Adults need to supervise sand play to make sure that sand is not thrown. Children with long, oiled or very curly hair should be encouraged sensitively to tie it back, cover it with a scarf, or wear a shower cap.
- Younger children need little or no tools in the sand, as they get great sensory enjoyment through using their hands to mould and feel the sand. When equipment is used for certain experiences, it needs to be part of the overall curriculum plan. There should also be some opportunity for children to choose and experiment on their own.
- All equipment should be clean and in good condition. It should be stored where it is visible to the children, and could be classified according to the type of activity planned. There should be enough equipment provided so that all the children at the tray can participate.
- Children should be encouraged to wash their hands after playing with sand.
- Children should be involved in clearing away and sweeping up at the end of the session.

Activity

You are responsible for planning an activity with sand for 4-year-old children.
1 What would you choose?
2 How would this benefit their all-round development?

VALUE TO AREAS OF DEVELOPMENT AND LEARNING

Physical
Dry sand: pouring sand and filling containers develops arm muscles and hand-eye coordination. Dexterity is needed to handle tools correctly. Wet sand: control is needed when making moulds.

Social and moral
Sharing, planning and cooperating with other children is encouraged. Accepting and understanding the need for rules is reinforced. Children often make new friends whilst playing on the beach or in the sandpit in the local park.

Emotional
A relaxing therapeutic activity, sand play allows for release of aggression. It is enjoyable and often associated with beach holidays or playing in the park. There is no right or wrong way to use sand.

Intellectual
New concepts can be learnt (especially with the involvement of an adult and suitable equipment), such as light and heavy, full and empty. It is the perfect material for experimentation, exploration and aiding concentration, and leads to imaginative play. Sand makes links with their physical environment, and can be used in construction work, making homes and buildings. Making patterns and marks in sand is linked to early literacy.

Language
Sand gives opportunities to express needs, communicate decisions, and learn new vocabulary, such as 'gritty' or 'sifting'.

Aesthetic and spiritual
The wonder of the natural world can be appreciated with freedom to express creative ideas and feelings. Making patterns in sand is creative and aesthetic.

Sensory
Dry sand is a tactile experience, particularly digging your toes in to an outside sand area. Children learn about the properties of sand through the senses, and particularly through touching it. Tasting should be discouraged at all costs!

Clay

Like sand, clay is not usually played with at home. It is messy and needs the adult to have a relaxed attitude to the amount of mess it can make, otherwise some of the value of the material is lost. Children enjoy venting their aggression on clay, and it is particularly suitable for children who are upset or angry as it can be destroyed without incurring adult disapproval. Clay can be handled harshly, bashed about, and will always resume its original form. It can be used very wet, and is then soothing and enjoyable.

Children proceed through different stages in their use of clay. At first they explore and experiment, then they repeat their experiments and practise handling the material and this leads on to controlled use and creativity. From the age of about four, it may be used as a modelling material.

In most establishments, terracotta or grey clay is used. There are other types, such as New Clay which sets very hard and does not need firing.

AMOUNT OF SPACE		TYPE OF SPACE	
Whole area		Outside	■
Half area		Inside	■
Quarter area		Hard surface	■
Small area	■	Carpeted	
		Table space	■

TYPE OF PLAY		INVOLVEMENT OF ADULT	
Solitary	■	Essential	
Parallel	■	Enriching	■
Small group	■	Not always necessary	■
Large group		Can be intrusive	■

ESSENTIAL MATERIALS
Clay
Water
Protective clothing
Storage bin
Space for drying

ADDITIONAL EQUIPMENT
Modelling and cutting tools
Rolling pins and wooden mallets
Artifacts for printing in clay, such as natural materials: shells, pine cones, pebbles; and construction equipment such as Lego bricks, Sticklebricks etc.
Bowls of water with different sponges

Good Practice

- It is particularly important to keep clay in good condition, as it quickly becomes dry and unusable, but properly stored can be re-used for many years. Store it in a bin with a well-fitting lid. Before putting clay away in the bin, knead it into a round or square shape, and insert water in a hole made by the thumb. If clay does dry out, immerse it in a bucket of water, allow it to soften and you may then remould it. Try to prevent different types of clay being mixed together. The coolest part of the room is the best place to keep the clay bin. Rigid containers can be used for small amounts of clay – far safer than using plastic bags.
- Clay should be available every day.
- Children may need encouraging to work with clay. It is a good idea for you to sit at the table with the children, manipulating the clay, showing enjoyment. Even if it is not possible to position an adult at the clay table all the time, close supervision is necessary as clay can become very messy indeed if too much water is added. This would not matter if you were using the clay outside. Children's clothing must be well protected, and hands washed after play. Inside, it is sensible to put newspapers on the floor.
- A bucket of soapy water with a cloth or two in it is a good idea, as some children get upset if their hands are covered in clay.
- When children are first introduced to clay, there should not be any tools or equipment offered, as these tend to get in the way of sensory experiences.
- Equipment offered to more experienced children should be planned to connect with the curriculum. All tools should be in good condition and easily accessible. Give children the opportunity occasionally to plan their own activities.
- Not all children are drawn to clay, therefore you will be seen as a role model whilst displaying enthusiasm for this material. Never make models for the children to copy, even if they beg you to. This would interfere with their own creativity, as they would take your model as setting the standard.

VALUE TO AREAS OF DEVELOPMENT AND LEARNING

Physical
Clay strengthens arm and finger muscles and promotes manipulative skills.

Social and moral
Clay is often played with in a small group. It encourages children to share equipment and ideas. Children should help in clearing up afterwards. Children may explore how clay is used by different cultures, for example in cooking and lighting equipment. Clay also develops a respect for other children's creations.

Emotional
It allows children to vent their feelings, particularly those of anger and frustration. When wet it is particularly relaxing and therapeutic. Initially there does not have to be an end product, so clay is a non-judgemental experience.

Intellectual
Many mathematical experiences can be offered to children, for example Piaget's conservation tests (see Hobart C. and Frankel J., *A Practical Guide to Child Observation and Assessment*, 2nd edition, Stanley Thornes (Publishers) Ltd, 1999). Opportunities arise for joint planning and decision making when children are constucting large models with other children. Clay may be linked with museum trips to see artifacts made of clay, and a visit to a potter. It can link in with curriculum projects on buildings and houses.

Language
Using clay encourages a range of vocabulary, such as 'malleable', 'mould' etc. Children in a group will discuss what they are making.

Aesthetic and spiritual
Clay is a natural material which inspires creativity and encourages an appreciation of other children's work.

Sensory
Clay is a wonderfully tactile experience.

Activity

Plan a class project for 7-year-olds, using clay. In what ways would your project develop their intellectual ability?

Mud

Once children are mobile, most of them find out about mud quite quickly, and should be allowed to play with it outside freely if suitably dressed and fully immunised. You will need to check that the garden is free from pesticides. Establishments should enquire of caregivers as to whether their children are protected against tetanus. Mud is one of the most enjoyable of natural materials for young children and is free and readily available in every garden. Mud can be mixed with water to give enjoyable sensory experiences, and can be seen to dry out to revert to dry soil. Small animals found in the mud give interest and pleasure to children, who often need to be persuaded to return them to their natural habitat.

Plasticine

This useful manufactured material is good for developing manipulative skills, and for making models with older children. It is much cleaner and less messy than other malleable materials and is often familiar to children from their play at home but it is not nearly as versatile or as tactile as other malleable materials. It can get hard very easily and needs storing in a warm environment. The colours tend to get mixed together, becoming a uniform sludge. This should no longer be used by the children for modelling, but is very useful in propping up 3D displays, and in floating and sinking experiments.

Dough

Dough can be made in many ways and presented to children in a range of colours, and the children will enjoy participating in the mixing. By adding other ingredients, apart from the essential flour and water, different kinds of elasticity can be achieved. Salt should always be added as a preservative, and it will also ensure that children do not eat it. Dough should appear attractive, have enough elasticity without sticking to surfaces or fingers, and should last for at least a week in a sealed plastic container, kept in a cool place. Playing with dough is a relaxing, soothing social activity, and is one often chosen by children when settling in to a new environment. Conversations around the dough table often stimulate a shy child to take part, as the experience helps relaxation. It can also be used in role play, and when baked and painted can be used to make models of food, in the same way as clay.

Activity

Investigate at home, experimenting with different dough recipes using various flours, ingredients and colours. Record the one you found most successful.
  Having experienced this yourself, you might like to involve the children at your placement in predicting and experimenting with various recipes.

Wood

Wood can be used either in the form of sawdust, and experimented with in a similar way to dry sand, or as offcuts of wood on a woodwork bench. All offcuts will need sanding down before use. Using wood to make models is a suitable activity for the older children in the group, but necessitates the presence of an adult to supervise the use of potentially dangerous tools. Tools should be scaled down versions of adult tools, and not toy ones. There is no value in a plastic hammer or screwdriver. Children need to have careful and repeated explanations of the dangers of woodwork tools. This is a useful activity to present outside as the noise from banging and hammering is less intrusive.

Activity

Using the standard headings (as on pages 11, 15 and 18), outline the value of working with wood to each area of development and learning.

Essential points

Equal opportunities

- Natural and malleable materials are enjoyed by all age groups and are culture and gender-free experiences.
- Natural materials can be linked to themes looking at how materials are used throughout the world.
- Boys can be encouraged in washing dolls and dolls' clothes, using dolls and clothes from a wide range of ethnic groups.
- Water, wood and sand encourage girls to use scientific equipment and tools and to become interested in technology and this should be reinforced by the staff team.
- Disabled children particularly benefit from play with these materials, as an end product is not required, and all the experiences are pleasurable and therapeutic, increasing self-esteem and confidence.

Safety

- Dry sand is often a hazard and needs careful supervision and thus is generally unsuitable for under threes. The floor needs to be swept regularly. Children should not be allowed to throw sand as this can cause choking, painful irritation in the eyes, and is difficult to remove from tight curly hair.
- All children playing with any volume of water need constant observation and supervision, as drowning can occur very quickly. If children are playing with ice outside, they also need to be closely supervised as ice is dangerous if thrown.
- The floor must be mopped frequently to prevent falls on a slippery surface.
- If plastic bags are used for storing clay, they must be too small to go over children's heads and should not be left around.

- Proper tools should be used when at the woodwork bench, as toy tools do not work properly and cause frustration. Therefore the bench must be supervised at all times, the correct tools used for the job, and instruction given in the right way to use the tools. These must be kept in good condition and stored carefully when not in use. The number of children at the bench needs to be limited so that the adult can be sure that mishaps will not take place.
- Children should be discouraged from eating dough.

Resources

Evans D. and Williams C., 1994, *Water and Floating*, Dorling Kindersley Ltd.

Gibson R. and Tyler J., 1989, *Playdough*, You and Your Child Series, Usborne Publishing.

Harpley A. and Roberts A., 1996, *Water and Sand*, Learning Through Play Series, Scholastic.

Henderson A., 1993, *Wood Play*, PLA.

Morris J., 1997, *Water*, Themes for Early Years Series, Scholastic.

Steen P. ét al., 1984, *Woodworking for Young Children*, National Association for the Education of Young Children.

Have Fun with Plasticine, Phaidon Press Ltd, 1993

Sand and Water, Clay and Dough, PPA Learn Through Play Series, PPA

3 Cooking

From a very young age, children enjoy watching and helping adults prepare and cook food. Food is a primary need, and encouraging children to
cook and prepare food at home, and later in a pre-school group, helps to
develop a sensory pleasure in food, which is such an important element of
life. Children learn about food hygiene and balanced meals, how to make
choices in the supermarkets for taste and value, and where different foods
come from.

It is possible today to buy food from all around the world, and by using
recipes from other countries children learn about different cultures in a most
enjoyable way. Children and parents who were not born in this country feel
valued and at home when an important part of their culture is recognised.

'Cooking' covers a wide range of activities in the classroom, from making a sandwich to producing a complicated meal. Unlike most experiences introduced in the pre-school, cooking has an end product. It therefore follows that the adult has to be more involved, and needs to direct the children to a certain extent. For this reason, it is even more important that the children do as much as possible for themselves, being involved from the preparation stage through to sharing the end product, and thought must be given as to which foods are suitable for group cooking.

AMOUNT OF SPACE		TYPE OF SPACE	
Whole area		Outside	
Half area		Inside	■
Quarter area		Hard surface	■
Small area	■	Carpeted	
		Table space	■
TYPE OF PLAY		**INVOLVEMENT OF ADULT**	
Solitary	■	Essential	■
Parallel		Enriching	
Small group	■	Not always necessary	
Large group		Can be intrusive	

ESSENTIAL MATERIALS

Protective clothing, preferably used only for cooking

Floor mop

Range of good quality cooking utensils, such as bowls, plates, forks, knives, spoons of various sizes, baking trays, saucepans

Hot water, for clearing up afterwards

Recipe and ingredients

SUGGESTED ADDITIONAL EQUIPMENT

Kettle

Access to an oven or microwave, and to a fridge; oven gloves for adult

Scales

A rotary whisk

A sieve

VALUE TO AREAS OF DEVELOPMENT AND LEARNING

Physical
Cooking develops large muscles in the arms when pouring, rolling, kneading, stirring, mixing and whisking, and in lifting trays, bowls and tins. It involves fine and gross manipulative skills, such as measuring, spooning liquids and solids, cracking eggs, decorating buns, cutting up fruit and vegetables, making sandwiches.

Social and moral
When children work cooperatively in a group, they share utensils, equipment and food, take turns, develop awareness of different eating patterns and cultural diversity and learn the need to clear away efficiently. Safety rules have to be learnt and followed.

Emotional
Cooking gives independence through the ability to cook for oneself. 7-year-olds can follow a recipe, working together, and only need support from an adult. Cooking promotes pride and self-esteem and, although not all children wish to eat what they have cooked, the activity nevertheless produces a valued end product. It is an enjoyable reminder of home. Tension is released when beating, kneading and whipping food.

Intellectual
By helping to plan the activity, children gain shopping skills such as making lists, choosing ingredients and handling money. Listening to and following instructions aids concentration. Cooking enforces a range of mathematical and scientific concepts, such as weighing, measuring, recognition of number, volume, expansion and contraction, fractions, sequencing, density, temperature, etc. Cooking promotes an understanding of nutritional principles, home safety and hygiene. Recipes and labelling make links with reading and writing as does the recognition of different scripts if the food is labelled in a different language. Knowledge of foods from many cultures will be gained, and children from the age of 6 will begin to follow recipes from a book. They will begin to understand basic nutrition and healthy eating patterns.

Language
Children will have to listen carefully in order to gain new vocabulary, such as 'dissolving', 'freezing', 'liquid' and 'solid'. They will also learn correct mathematical and scientific terms, express their needs, ask questions and consult with adults.

Aesthetic and spiritual

Children enjoy the apparent 'magical' changes due to food combinations and temperature. They learn about the attractive presentation of food and of links between food and religious and cultural festivals.

Sensory

It can be an overwhelming sensory experience involving taste, smell, touch, sight and sounds.

Good Practice

- All food must be very fresh and in excellent condition, and dried goods stored in airtight containers. Utensils must be scrupulously clean, and table tops wiped with hot soapy water and a clean cloth before use. Hands need to be washed, and nails scrubbed. Long hair should be tied back. Children with colds, sores or cuts should be excluded from the activity until well.
- Aprons should be used just for cooking. It is useful to have a clean cloth and a bowl of hot soapy water available in case of spills.
- A range of cooking activities should be offered to the children, from simple jelly making, which shows how heat changes food, to more complicated recipes such as mixing several ingredients. Parents are a useful resource for information concerning food preparation and recipes.
- All cooking activities have value, but the most important thing for the children is to be involved in every aspect of the experience, if possible from discussing what they are about to cook, to shopping for the ingredients, preparing the equipment, producing the food, washing and clearing up, and relating what they have achieved to the rest of the class, who should also take part in eating. Enough food should be cooked so that the whole group can enjoy the end product.
- The activity should be organised so that children do not have to handle very hot liquids, and only the adult uses the oven.
- Nearly all children enjoy cooking, so you must make sure that it takes place often, and that all children have a turn. To ensure that children get the most from the experience, four is the maximum number, and this can be achieved by having only four cooking aprons, and adhering strictly to a rota system. Try to avoid always cooking sweet food, as this is an opportunity for children to try out new tastes and develop a more sophisticated palate. The constant presence of an adult is needed, for safety and hygiene reasons, to answer and ask questions, to foster language development, to encourage manipulative skills and to ensure fair turn-taking.
- Careful planning and preparation is necessary, thought being given to age-appropriate experiences.

Essential points

Equal opportunities

- Cooking is an experience enjoyed equally by boys and girls and presents an opportunity for them to work together. Avoid making stereotypical assumptions about gender and racial preferences.
- When deciding on a cooking activity, check that no child is prevented from participating due to cultural or religious diet prohibitions.
- Sharing food experiences and different utensils from around the world shifts children away from an ethnocentric perception of food preparation. It offers many opportunities for making traditional dishes and linking in with cultural and religious festivals.
- Cooking is especially valuable for children/young adults who have special needs or learning disabilities as it encourages independence and self-reliance. Care must be taken to ensure that no child is allergic to anything you wish to cook, or that it contravenes a special diet.

Activity

Plan a party for a group of 7-year-olds where the children are involved in the planning and preparation of the food.

Safety

- Close supervision is essential at all times. Preparation must be very thorough, and it is important to have all the necessary equipment and ingredients to hand so as not to leave the children unattended. Cooker guards must be used if the oven is in the same room as the children and they need to be taught about the dangers of heat, and how to handle sharp knives safely. An adult should always put food in and out of the oven, and the rules of safety should be frequently stated and observed through good role modelling.
- No wires should be allowed to trail on the floor.
- Any spills on the floor should be mopped up immediately to avoid accidents.
- A first aid box should be nearby in case of cuts or burns.
- A fire extinguisher and a fire blanket must be kept near the oven.
- Potentially dangerous items of equipment should be stored out of the way of children, and put away immediately after use.

Resources

Benjamin F., 1988, *Caribbean Food*, Exploring Food in Britain Series, Mantra Publishing Ltd.

Clark L., 1998, *Food*, Themes for Early Years Series, Scholastic.

De Boo M., 1990, *Science Activities*, Bright Ideas for Early Years Series, Scholastic Publications Ltd.

Drew H., 1994, *My First Baking Book*, Dorling Kindersley Ltd.

Dunbar, K., 1992, *The Spice of Life*, Belair.

Edwards N., 1995, *Food*, Messages Series, A. & C. Black (Publishers) Ltd.

Hill S. E., 1990, *More Than Rice and Peas*, The Food Commission.

Husain S., 1988, *Indian Food*, Exploring Food in Britain Series, Mantra Publishing Ltd.

Lim J., 1990, *Chinese Food*, Exploring Food in Britain Series, Mantra Publishing Ltd.

Lynn S. and James D., 1992, *I Can Make It: Fun Food*, Two-Can Publishing.

Robins D., 1994, *The Kids Round the World Cookbook*, Kingfisher Books.

Whiting M. and Lobstein T., 1992, *The Nursery Food Book*, Edward Arnold.

Wilkes A., 1987, *First Cookbook*, Usborne Publishing, and 1994, *The Children's Step By Step Cookbook*, Dorling Kindersley Ltd.

Wilkins V., 1990, *Cookery Cards for Children*, Tamarind Books.

Young C., 1992, *Round the World Cookbook*, Usborne Publishing.

Cooking Round the World, PPA Learn Through Play Series, Ealing PPA.

4　*Imaginary Play*

Imaginary play grows out of imitative play. Babies from a very early age imitate adults in games of 'peek-a-boo', waving goodbye and copying actions. Later, children do not need a direct role model in front of them, but will start to use their memory, pouring out imaginary cups of tea for all and sundry, and pretending to eat non-existent food.

At around 2½ years, children start to take on roles. One will be the 'mummy', and another the 'daddy', and this will gradually extend to include the baby, the big sister, and even a visiting aunt. As children become older, role play will be extended to other people familiar in their lives or from books, such as the nurse, and the firefighter. The provision of dressing-up clothes often stimulates the imagination of the children. It is best to provide clothes that can be used in many different ways, the only exception being those used in the hospital corner, where children need a more realistic environment to allay their fears.

In the pre-school environment, domestic play, such as family roles, mealtimes, bedtimes and so on, is carried out in the Home Area. This activity gives a great deal of comfort to the young child, particularly those starting school or nursery.

Although discouraged in most homes and pre-school establishments, and to the despair of many parents and teachers, children do have imaginary shoot-outs, but they do not need toy guns, Lego bricks will do just as well. But it is from this ability to symbolise inanimate objects that the readiness for reading grows, as a child starts to understand that those inky blobs on a page stand for real words in a story.

For some children, acting out a role can be a release of emotions through pretending to be someone else. A child who is constantly listening to adults quarrelling may find it helpful to pretend to be one of those adults, and have some say of their own. This type of play can give you an insight into possible difficulties at home, but caution must be exercised, as the children could be acting out what they have seen on the television the night before. On the other hand, never disregard what a child might be trying to tell you, until it has been completely checked out and discussed with your supervisor. Observations will come in very useful here, as it will give you an opportunity of discussing the child with your supervisor, who may have more knowledge of the child's background.

A child waiting to go into hospital will find it very useful to be a make-believe patient, as a way of expressing emotions and fears.

Some children, who may be withdrawn or shy, may still have difficulty in expressing their emotions. Puppets can be a great help here, as the child uses them to voice hidden feelings. Ready made puppets should be introduced cautiously, as small children can be fearful of a toy that seems to have a life of its own. Far better to get the children to make their own puppets, even if they are only made from a cereal box or a paper bag.

As children are small, vulnerable people, they enjoy acting out roles of super-heroes. It makes them feel empowered and strong, and is a boost to their self-esteem.

Children play with dolls in different ways at each stage of their development. Once babies start to walk, they will use the doll as any other inanimate object, just holding onto it anywhere (usually the feet) and dragging it after them. At about 2 years, some children will start to cuddle the doll, treating it more as a baby, particularly if there has been a recent birth in the family. This baby might come in for some very hard knocks! A little later on, children enjoy bathing dolls, dressing (but mainly undressing) dolls and taking them out for walks in a push-chair. At about 6 years, groups of children might play with several dolls, having pretend tea parties or schoolrooms. Many girls and boys start to collect dolls, such as Barbie and Action Man, and there is often rivalry in the collecting of their clothes and artefacts.

Small scale models of people, animals, vehicles, dolls houses, and items of domestic equipment are often used in imaginary play. They are familiar to the children, and the play allows them to relax, and extend and develop language.

These toys can be used in conjunction with other equipment in the nursery or school classroom, such as the sand tray and the home corner.

For some imaginary activities, it is best to use the real equipment; for example, when setting up a hairdresser's salon, a dentist's surgery, or a hospital ward, the proper tools of the trade are readily available, and add more to the play. You obviously do not provide the more dangerous equipment!

You will become aware that more imaginary play takes place when there are fewer directed activities. With the permission of your supervisor, you might like to try the experiment of providing nothing for the children for the first half hour or so, and note how the children are able to amuse themselves, mainly in imaginary play.

AMOUNT OF SPACE		TYPE OF SPACE	
Whole area		Outside	■
Half area	■	Inside	■
Quarter area	■	Hard surface	■
Small area	■	Carpeted	■
		Table space	■
TYPE OF PLAY		**INVOLVEMENT OF ADULT**	
Solitary	■	Essential	
Parallel	■	Enriching	■
Small group	■	Not always necessary	■
Large group	■	Can be intrusive	■

ESSENTIAL MATERIALS
None

SUGGESTED ADDITIONAL MATERIALS
Home Corner and domestic play equipment
Small world toys
Dressing-up clothes, particularly hats, wigs and pieces of material and clothing
  worn by different cultural groups, such as saris, shalwar kameez and Chinese
  slippers
Dolls, and dolls clothes
Puppets
Empty cardboard boxes and cartons
Wooden blocks

Good Practice

- Imaginary play is sometimes undervalued, but time, space and opportunity should be provided every day. Constant observation will ensure that you facilitate and extend such opportunities.
- All equipment should be kept in good order, and children can help with this. Clothes should be hung on hangers, cleaned and repaired routinely, and removed once this is no longer possible. There should be enough dressing-up materials to allow different themes to be acted out, and for every child to have access to something. Clothing from all cultures should be treated with respect, and the adult team should be knowledgeable in the correct naming and wearing of clothing, such as saris and turbans. Parents and friends could be encouraged to lend or give clothing, so that there is always some in reserve. Be aware, however, that some parents may lend something of great sentimental value, so always check with parents that they understand the object may be damaged in the play.
- On occasion, parents might feel anxious if their child is taking on a role of which they disapprove. Try and involve parents in the play, and explain how valuable such play can be.
- Some imaginary play can be repetitious, such as that based on television characters. The intervention of an adult can often add a new dimension to the play.
- The role of the adult is a sensitive one in imaginative play. Children need their privacy, and the opportunity to develop the play in their own way. Adults should wait to be invited, and should then see themselves as an equal participant, not a dominant one. Sensitively adding new vocabulary to the conversation aids language development. Knowing that children might be facing a particular difficulty, such as the birth of a new baby, or hospital admission, you can help a great deal, by setting up an environment in which babies can be cared for, or hospital procedures carried out. Fear of the dentist or the barber can be allayed by make-belive play in the 'surgery' or the 'hairdresser'.

VALUE TO AREAS OF DEVELOPMENT AND LEARNING

Physical
Imaginary play can be very energetic, particularly when enacting super-heroes/heroines. Large muscles are used when dressing up. Manipulative skills and hand-eye coordination are used in fastening clothes, dressing dolls, handling domestic equipment, and in playing with small world toys.

Social and moral
Imaginary play allows children to experience the roles of others. Children often play together in large and small groups, as some imaginary games need social interaction. Children have to take turns and share equipment. It allows children to display caring and social skills: e.g, nursing, parenting and showing hospitality, and encourages children to explore different cultural backgrounds in the use of multicultural domestic equipment and clothes. Children start to form their own identity through role/imaginary play.

Emotional
Imaginary play allows children to express and release positive and negative emotions. It gives confidence, and allows self-esteem to develop. Playing roles empowers children, and lets them glimpse and begin to come to terms with the adult world. Domestic play is a link with home, and very comforting to the insecure child, or a child experiencing a new situation. Playing with dolls can allow a child to express negative feelings, without harm to a new addition to the family.

Intellectual
Domestic play offers mathematical experiences in matching and sorting and one-to-one correspondence, by laying tables and putting crockery and cutlery away in the correct place. Graded dolls and dolls' clothes help children understand concepts of small, medium and large, and can give children a range of mathematical experiences. Doll play can lead on to discussion about reproduction and childcare. Imaginary play presents opportunities for children to direct and organise activities, promotes creativity, and may lead to writing imaginative stories. It also aids problem-solving by encouraging a child to invent new ways of doing things.

Language

It stimulates language and the use of new vocabulary, particularly with the involvement of a sympathetic and sensitive adult. Imaginary play promotes discussion on life experiences.

Aesthetic and spiritual

Imaginary play presents opportunities to participate in other cultures, and encourages an appreciation of other children's life experiences.

Sensory

Rich materials give tactile experiences, for example in handling clothing and fabrics.

Essential points

Equal opportunities

- You may see children using stereotypes in their role play, copying situations observed in their environment. You will have to challenge this behaviour in a sensitive way. Imaginary play allows boys to take on and dress up in perceived female roles such as the mother or the ballerina, whilst girls can be fathers and firefighters. Sometimes boys need to be encouraged to use the Home Corner, as this may be seen as the girls' domain.
- Equipment, clothes and pretend food from many cultures should be provided in the Home Corner. Dolls and small world people should also reflect the multicultural world, with different skin tones and ethnic features.
- Children in wheelchairs should have access to the Home Corner.
- Children challenged in any special way need as much or more opportunity for imaginary play. This might necessitate more involvement on the part of the staff.
- Make sure the neck openings of dressing-up clothes are wide and that trousers are wide enough to fit over calipers. Some of your resources should reflect disability, such as puppets with hearing aids, or dolls in wheelchairs.

Safety

- Children enjoy wearing adult shoes, particularly high heels, as this not only gives them height, but a feeling of importance. They should never be allowed to wear such shoes outside, or with any climbing equipment. Clothes which are too long are a similar hazard. Clothing such as scarves, ties and belts draped around the neck is obviously dangerous. Some jewellery might have sharp pins or clasps, and bead necklaces can break and be swallowed.

■ When real equipment is used in make-believe play, such as the dentist's surgery, you will obviously provide only safe equipment, such as dental mirrors, toothbrushes and toothpaste. Electrical equipment, such as hairdryers or food mixers need to have plugs and wires removed before being used in play. The use of water needs to be monitored. All equipment must be checked regularly.

Activity

1 Observe children aged 2 years and 4 years playing with dolls. How does their behaviour differ?
2 Make a cloak from a piece of material gathered at one end with elastic. Do the boys and girls play with it in the same way?
3 Try to identify the different types of imaginary play that occur in the nursery/classroom. How much is spontaneous? How much is adult-directed?
4 Add an item to the Home Area to extend imaginative play. Observe the outcome.

Resources

Beckles Wilson R. and Gray L., 1993, *Just Imagine*, Blair.

Caudron C., Childs C. and Gibson L., 1993, *Dressing Up*, How To Make Series, Usborne Publishing.

Garnett S., 1996, *Home Corner*, Learning Through Play Series, Scholastic.

Gussein Paley V., 1984, *Superheroes in the Doll Corner*, University of Chicago.

Leach B., 1997, *Small World Play*, Learning through Play Series, Scholastic.

Scher A. and Verrall C., 1987, *100+ Ideas for Drama* and *Another 100+ Ideas for Drama*, Heinemann.

Make and Play, 1994, Early Learning Series, Zigzag Publications.
Make Believe Play, 1991, PPA Learn Through Play Series, PPA.

Galt supplies the Dara Doll and a set of calipers, crutches, spectacles and hearing aids. Galt, Brookfield Road, Cheadle, Cheshire SK8 2PN. Telephone 0161 428 8511

J. and M. Toys are specialists in dressing-up clothes, including clothes from around the world. J. and M. Toys, 46 Finsbury Drive, Wrose, Bradford, W. Yorks BD2 1QA. Telephone 01274 599 314

Ann Johnson, Multi-Ethnic Dolls and Puppets, 38 Gledhow Wood Grove, Leeds LS8 1NZ. Telephone 01532 667177

5 *Painting and Drawing*

This chapter covers spontaneous painting and drawing, carried out by young children, undirected by adults.

All children should be offered frequent opportunities to paint and draw when they feel inclined. When very young, before fluent speech, spontaneous painting and drawing is a most valuable means of expression. This is very much reduced if adults insist on questioning children about their paintings, suggest additions to the work, and want captions for every painting or drawing.

Adults interpreting children's paintings are quite often wrong. Children love to do all-dark one-colour paintings at some stage in their development – this does not mean that something terrible has happened to them that they wish to forget! Understanding what stage of development children might have reached through interpreting their paintings is interesting, and there are many books on this subject.

AMOUNT OF SPACE		TYPE OF SPACE	
Whole area		Outside	■
Half area		Inside	■
Quarter area	■	Hard surface	■
Small area	■	Carpeted	
		Table space	■
TYPE OF PLAY		**INVOLVEMENT OF ADULT**	
Solitary	■	Essential	
Parallel	■	Enriching	
Small group		Not always necessary	
Large group		Can be intrusive	■

ESSENTIAL MATERIALS

For painting:
Protection for clothing
Old newspapers for protecting the floor, the easel and the table top
A floor mop
Facilities for drying paintings
Paints, paper, brushes, clean water
For drawing:
Pencils and paper
Chubby crayons for the youngest children

SUGGESTED ADDITIONAL EQUIPMENT

For painting:
Large variety of paints and brushes
Different thicknesses of paint
Different materials, such as sand, to change the texture of the paint
Different sizes, textures, shapes and colours of paper
Non-spillable paint containers, and pots to mix colours in
A drying rack or line
For drawing:
Crayons, felt pens, pastels, chalks and charcoal.
Chalkboards
Different sizes, textures, shapes and colours of paper

Good Practice

■ Painting is a messy activity, which is why it is not always done in the home, and therefore young children should be given every opportunity to explore this medium undisturbed whenever they wish.

- Aprons in good condition should be provided.
- Tables, easels and the floor should be covered in newspaper and cleaned regularly. A mop and bucket should be placed nearby and the children should have easy access to the bathroom.
- The children will get the most from painting and drawing if they are left to pursue it on their own. Adults should not interrupt, ask questions about the picture, or make suggestions. They should never paint or draw for the child, or impose their ideas and concepts. Children will think the adult interpretation to be the superior one, and this will discourage them from valuing their own work and may stunt their creativity. Outline or character shapes should never be provided for the children.
- The activity should be presented attractively, and sited where the light is good. Paints should be of a creamy consistency and mixed freshly every day. The children might want to help with this. There should be a good range of colours, and each paintpot should have its own brush so as to keep the colours clear and bright. All drawing materials should be in good condition, and there should be enough provided.
- There should be a choice of paper, placed so that the children can help themselves. A drying area for paintings is a necessity.
- It is obtrusive to some children to put their name on their paintings and drawings. Always ask the child first. Children usually do not want to take their work home; once they have done the activity it has no more interest for them. Nursery staff insisting on paintings and drawings going home risk the children's disappointment if the parent/carer does not value the work sufficiently.
- Only add captions if the child asks you to, and use the child's words.
- Drawing is not always a solitary activity, and friends often sit at a table and draw together. Children's drawings show developmental stages more clearly than paintings and are most useful to keep for recording purposes.
- A visit to an art gallery can be useful in generating interest and discussion.

Activity

Make a book of paintings and drawings by the children in the nursery or school, adding the ages, and showing clearly the different stages of development that the children have reached.

Discussion point
If you were asked to paint or draw a picture without being given a theme or title, would you be able to do this? Identify any areas of difficulty. Why do you think children can do it so naturally?

VALUE TO AREAS OF DEVELOPMENT AND LEARNING

Physical
Painting at the easel develops large muscles in the arms of the younger child. As the child gains more control, finer manipulative skills are developed, aiding hand-eye coordination.

Social and moral
Spontaneous painting is not a social activity.

Emotional
Painting, in particular, often allows children to express emotions that they find difficult to put into words. This is an enjoyable new activity for many young children on starting nursery. Attaining this skill leads to a sense of achievement and self-esteem.

Intellectual
Painting and drawing encourages imagination and creativity, and lends itself to pattern creation. The exploration of materials, textures and techniques expands knowledge of colour and shapes. It helps children to understand spatial relationships and composition.

Symbolic blobs lead to the foundation of reading and writing.

Language
This is not an experience which particularly develops language, but the child might want to discuss the painting or drawing with an adult or another child.

Aesthetic and spiritual
Painting and drawing develop an aesthetic awareness of composition, colour, shape, patterns and relationships.

Sensory
Good experiences for sensory development, especially of sight and touch are provided by painting and drawing.

Essential points

Equal opportunities

- Painting and drawing are essentially culture- and gender-free activities at the pre-school stage. Make sure that the range of colours allows children from all ethnic groups to represent themselves and their families realistically, should they want to do so.
- The National Curriculum dictates that children should develop an awareness of art from a young age. Care must be taken to show children the work of a wide range of artists, and not just that of European males.
- Children with disabilities will enjoy and learn a great deal from using painting and drawing materials. Care must be taken to make sure that all children have access to this experience. Standing frames can be used for motor-impaired children, to support them whilst painting.
- Visually-impaired children would benefit from tactile and fluorescent materials, and textured paper. Short stubby brushes are easier to handle.

Safety

- Very young children need watching to make sure they do not eat the paint. All paint used must be lead-free and non-toxic.
- Children should be discouraged from walking around with pencils or brushes in their mouths, or from chewing lead pencils.
- Remove pen tops when being used by very young children, to avoid the possibility of choking.
- Major spills should be mopped up quickly to avoid the possibility of falls.
- Hand washing after painting should be supervised.

Resources

Barnes R., 1987, *Teaching Art to Young Children 4–9 Years*, Routledge.
Cox M., 1992, *Children's Drawings*, Penguin.
De Boo M., 1995, *Colour*, Themes for Early Years Series, Scholastic.
FitzMaurice Mills J., 1991, *Art for All Our Children*, Wolfhound Press.
Gardner H., 1980, *Artful Scribbles*, Jill Norman.
Gibson R. and Barlow A., 1994, *What Shall I Draw?*, Usborne Publishing.
Goodnow J., 1980, *Children's Drawing*, Developing Child Series, Fontana.
Kellogg R., 1969, *Analysing Children's Art*, Mayfield Publishing Co.
Lasky L. and Mukherji R., 1980, *Art: Basics for Young Children*, National Association for the Education of Young Children, Washington DC.
Matthews J., 1994, *Helping Children to Draw and Paint in Early Childhood*, Hodder & Stoughton.
Micklethwaite L., 1993, A *Child's Book of Art*, Dorling Kindersley Ltd.
Strauss M., 1978, *Understanding Children's Drawings*, Rudolph Steiner Press.
Wolfe G., 1997, *The Children's Art Book*, Bellew Publishing.

6 *Creative Art Activities*

Under this heading we have grouped all activities which involve creative thought on the part of the child, but are generally adult directed. For example, the modelling of recycleable materials is dependent on the materials provided by the adult, and printing by the way the adult sets up the activity.

If children are allowed to use their own ideas within the constraints named above, creative art activities will stimulate their imagination and aesthetic awareness, encourage their creativity, aid social development by sharing materials and turn-taking, and develop language skills as the children have to understand instructions and ask questions. Many activities will link in with the curriculum.

Children usually work in small groups with an adult supervising, and sometimes the whole class is involved as part of a theme which is being explored.

The following list of suggestions for creative art activities is not a comprehensive list, by any means.

Printing

Activities could include printing with vegetables, fruits, sponges, Lego bricks, Sticklebricks, leaves and string using paints, inks and dyes. Hand and foot prints and toy cars can also be used.

Recyclable material modelling

Sometimes referred to as junk modelling, the activity can use all shapes and sizes of cartons, containers, pots and odds and ends, using different types of glue, paste, Blu-tack and sticky tape.

Painting

Butterfly prints, drip paintings, paintings in different shades of one colour, marble painting, oil painting, sugar painting, bubble painting, straw painting and making patterns are some suggestions.

Older children may be encouraged to draw objects, plants or animals in a realistic way.

Collage

Use paper of all kinds, such as tissue, sweet papers, postcards, magazine pictures and foil; other manufactured materials such as polystyrene chips, pieces of fabric, bottle tops and straws; and natural materials such as leaves, sand, twigs, seeds, shells, bark, wood and shavings.

Pasta and pulses can be used, but as with printing with food, some establishments might feel this is not ethically correct.

Messy play

Some activities provided for children are not adult directed in the same way. Messy play, such as playing with cooked spaghetti mixed with liquid detergent and colouring, or experimenting with cornflour and water which becomes solid in your hand, but liquid on a hard flat surface, is enjoyable for all children, but particularly so for the youngest ones. A large sheet of paper can be attached to the wall, and paint in squeezy bottles can be squirted at it. Finger painting comes into this category; paints and paste are mixed together, and patterns made in the mixture with the fingers. Older children might like to print their creations.

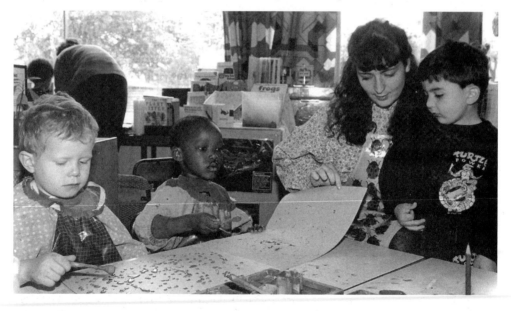

ESSENTIAL MATERIALS
Protection for clothing, the table top and the floor; floor mop and sponge
  for table spills
Facilities for drying work
Basin of water and towel to hand, to remove surplus materials
Other materials depend on chosen activity

AMOUNT OF SPACE		TYPE OF SPACE	
Whole area		Outside	■
Half area		Inside	■
Quarter area		Hard surface	■
Small area	■	Carpeted	
		Table space	■
TYPE OF PLAY		**INVOLVEMENT OF ADULT**	
Solitary	■	Essential	■
Parallel	■	Enriching	■
Small group	■	Not always necessary	
Large group	■	Can be intrusive	

Good Practice

- Most of the points made about good practice in the painting and drawing chapter remain true for creative art activities, with some additions.
- You should always prepare enough materials for all the children who wish to participate. This might not be possible during one session, but there is no reason not to repeat the activity later in the week.
- Some children might prefer not to be involved, and this should be respected.
- It becomes important for children to produce finished work as they progress through the infant school, but children under the age of 5 should be allowed just to explore the possibilities of the materials and take part at that level. If the expectation to always finish a creative art activity is stressed too much, some children might find taking part a negative experience.
- Although essentially adult directed, children can still be involved in choosing a creative activity, and these should be available at most sessions.
- Make sure all materials are kept in good order, especially those filling the junk box. Throw out materials that become torn or damaged. Discourage the use of insides of lavatory rolls, as these are obviously not hygienic.
- Before embarking on any creative art experience, make sure that it will be valuable to the child, and not just a way of keeping them busy on a wet Friday afternoon when you want to start on the weekend tidying up. Some activities, such as filling in an outline of a snowman with scrunched up pieces of white tissue paper, are of little value, and children take limited satisfaction in carrying out such useless tasks. Why not get them to help you wash the paint pots and the aprons instead: they will learn a great deal more from this than colouring in templates!
- Parents sometimes show concern that messy activities will spoil their children's clothes. Stains are more easily removed if a little washing up liquid is added to the paint.

VALUE TO AREAS OF DEVELOPMENT AND LEARNING

Physical
Creative art activities help children to develop arm muscles and fine manipulative skills leading to hand-eye coordination.

Social and moral
It helps children learn to share and take turns, working cooperatively on a group project, and understanding the rules of working in a group. For older children, a group project might provide a sense of identity.

Emotional
It provides enjoyment, a sense of achievement, and self-esteem.

Intellectual
One of the best activities for cognitive development, as children use their imagination and creativity in planning and producing this work. Concentration span is often extended in a well thought out enjoyable activity. Different materials encourage exploration and experimentation and this, in turn, leads to an understanding of design and technology. Mathematic and scientific concepts may be explored. Patterns may lead to understanding of spatial relationships. A sense of purpose is developed in older children in producing a piece of finished work.

Language
New vocabulary is learnt in different activities. Understanding instructions and asking questions develops comprehension and expressive speech.

Aesthetic and spiritual
These activities stimulate aesthetic awareness and the beginning of art appreciation, in pattern making, composition, use of colour and attractive materials. Creative art activities link in well with festivals and celebrations.

Sensory
Many of the materials and textures used will encourage tactile development, and colours will stimulate vision.

1 Plan a creative art activity with 6-year-old children. List the values of this activity to the areas of development.
2 Make a list of the creative art activities that take place in your establishment. Which ones most extend children's all-round development?

Essential points

Equal opportunities

- See previous chapter on painting and drawing.
- Blowing paint through a straw to make pictures develops mouth muscles and can help poor speech expression.
- Children with visual impairment should be encouraged to participate, using many different materials. They should not be forbidden the use of any tools, and they will need to be instructed in the correct use. They may need to work at an unusual angle.

Safety

- If very young children are involved or near the activity area, ensure they do not eat any of the materials, or insert any small objects into noses or ears.
- Before beginning bubble painting, ask the child to blow through the straw onto your hand.
- All materials which could be dangerous, such as scissors, need close supervision.
- Superglue should never be used, for obvious reasons.

Resources

Burgess L., 1994, *Art Activities*, Bright Ideas for Early Years Series, Scholastic Publications Ltd.

Chambers J. and Hood M., 1990, *Simply Artistic*, Belair Publications.

Davies J., 1992, *Technological Activities*, Bright Ideas for Early Years Series, Scholastic Publications Ltd.

Deshpande C., 1994, *Celebrations*, World Wide Crafts Series, A. & C. Black (Publishers) Ltd.

Einon D., 1996, *Creative Play*, Penguin.

Gadd T. and Morton D., 1992, *Technology Key Stage 1*, Blueprint Series, Stanley Thornes (Publishers) Ltd.

Gibson R., 1992, *Paint Fun*, You and Your Child Series, Usborne Publishing.

Gibson R. and Tyler J., 1990, *Paper Play*, You and Your Child Series, Usborne Publishing.

Hart T., 1979, *Make it with Hart*, Piccolo.

Leach B., 1997, *Junk Materials*. Learning Through Play Series, Scholastic.

Perkins S., 1998, *Seeing, making, doing: Creative Development in Early Years Settings*, National Early Years Network.

Sharman L., 1992, *Amazing Book of Shapes*, Dorling Kindersley Ltd.

Sharpe S., 1990, *Activity Time*, Jade Publishers.

Wolfe G., 1997, *The Children's Activity Book*, Bellew Publishing.

Glue, Crayon, Paint and *Scissors*, 1994, Five-minute Art Ideas Series, Zigzag Publishing.

Glueing, 1991, PPA Learn Through Play Series, PPA.

7 Small and Large Construction

Blocks

A bag of bricks is the most versatile piece of equipment that any child can use from the age of 1 year onwards. In nurseries and classrooms children have the opportunity of using many different types of blocks: from very large hollow ones that children can stand and climb on, to small ones such as Lego. Blocks can be hard and made out of wood or plastic, they can be soft and manufactured from rubber, cotton or foam, they can be brightly coloured or in natural wood – but they are all construction toys and are there to build with.

At first, children will play on their own, building a tower of bricks, and enjoying knocking it down again. This leads on to 4-year-olds planning small and large constructions together, playing cooperatively and imaginatively.

In the establishment in which you are working, you will probably have wooden blocks that are all units of each other. For example, two rectangular blocks laid together horizontally will make a square, as will four of the small square blocks.

Understanding these relationships aids children in mathematical concepts, particularly those of fractions and of shape. The way the bricks are stored is important, and children will soon learn how many of the smaller bricks are equal to the larger ones.

The youngest children will use bricks to build towers and walls, enjoying the destruction as much or more than the building. Children of 4 and 5 will start to build, and often decide what their construction is as it takes shape. Older children will plan their constructions first, choose the most suitable materials and refer to resource material for inspiration and information. 7-year-olds will use unit blocks to solve mathematical problems, and construction sets for developing and understanding technology.

Construction sets

There are very many types of construction sets on the market, the best known being Lego. Most children will be familiar with Lego from home, and it is probably the most versatile of the construction toys. Younger children will find Duplo (the large scale version) easier to put together. Older children, from 5 years upwards, enjoy Meccano, the wooden and plastic types being easier to manage than the metal, which is more sophisticated. There is an increasingly expanding market in construction sets, and you need to be assured of the value and versatility of each set before ordering.

AMOUNT OF SPACE		TYPE OF SPACE	
Whole area		Outside	■
Half area		Inside	■
Quarter area	■	Hard surface	■
Small area	■	Carpeted	■
		Table space	■
TYPE OF PLAY		**INVOLVEMENT OF ADULT**	
Solitary	■	Essential	
Parallel	■	Enriching	■
Small group	■	Not always necessary	■
Large group	■	Can be intrusive	■

ESSENTIAL MATERIALS
Bricks/blocks/construction sets and suitable storage

SUGGESTED ADDITIONAL MATERIALS
Model cars, animals and people
Blankets to make shelters
Large cardboard cartons

Good Practice

- Bricks and blocks should always be readily available for the children and stored somewhere they can reach for themselves. They must be kept in good condition and regularly checked for splinters. Plain wooden blocks will need to be varnished from time to time, especially if used outside. Plastic and foam blocks should be washed regularly. Construction sets need to be kept clean, and most are easy to wash. There need to be enough pieces, so that more than one child can play at the same time.
- Involve children in clearing away, so that they learn how to stack the blocks in the smallest possible space, as this will teach them how the sizes relate to each other. Labelling the area may help them. Bricks and blocks can be usefully stored in large drawstring bags.
- Children benefit from building their constructions in a large area, and if possible, a carpeted part of the room should be kept for bricks and blocks. It may occasionally be possible to leave the work set up so that the children can return to it later. Staff need to realise that group building may take some time and to give ample warning before asking the children to clear away.
- Books showing pictures of buildings, machines, space equipment, and forms of transport should be sited near the brick corner to aid the imagination.
- Adults should show sensitivity and understand when a child needs to work alone to solve problems, and anticipate when to offer help or extend the activity.

Activity

1 Using catalogues, list the different types of bricks, blocks and construction sets.
2 Which types would you find the most appropriate for children with special needs?
3 Which types would make the most complicated constructions?

VALUE TO AREAS OF DEVELOPMENT AND LEARNING

Physical
Large blocks promote good muscle development through lifting, carrying, stretching and balancing, while small bricks and construction sets aid gross and fine manipulative skills and hand-eye coordination.

Social and moral
Cooperation is needed when planning and building constructions in a group. Children may have to share and take turns. An activity may involve an adult working alongside children.

Emotional
This is an enjoyable activity which promotes a sense of achievement and self-esteem. It has a home-school link. Children can have an outlet for aggression by banging and breaking down a construction. Building life-size models leads to a feeling of being in control.

Intellectual
Building with bricks is a first hand experience of three-dimensional objects and spatial relationships. Many mathematical concepts are learnt such as height, weight, matching, sorting, and symmetry. It encourages concentration, creative thought and problem solving. For older children, using resource books will encourage literacy.

Language
Children have to understand and issue instructions when building together. Older children will need to read and follow instructions in planning and building more sophisticated models. Discussion of constructions with an adult will extend the children's language and learning.

Aesthetic and spiritual
A well-designed construction is a creative experience and the beginning of an appreciation of architecture and design.

Sensory
Polished wood gives a tactile experience.

Essential points

Equal opportunities

- Boys often dominate the brick corner. Posters in this area depicting both genders involved in construction work should be displayed.
- Staff may need to actively encourage girls to use this area of the class, even occasionally excluding the boys for a session. (The girls could be banned from the Home Corner for the same session.) The presence of an adult in the brick area will often encourage girls to participate.
- Children with special needs should have access to block play. Foam blocks are especially suitable. They may find it easier to play at a table and, if so, put a rug on the surface to prevent pieces slipping off.

Safety

- Large or heavy wooden blocks can be dangerous if thrown or allowed to topple onto other children.
- Wooden blocks need to be checked regularly for splinters.
- Small pieces from construction sets might make young children choke if they are put in the mouth.

Resources

Donati P., 1993, *Amazing Buildings*, Dorling Kindersley Ltd.

Edwards N., 1995, *Buildings*, Messages Series, A. & C. Black (Publishers) Ltd.

Evans D. and Williams C., 1993, *Building Things*, Let's Explore Science Series, Dorling Kindersley Ltd.

Gura P., 1992, *Exploring Learning: Young Children and Block Play*, Paul Chapman.

Heald C., 1997, *Construction Play*, Learning Through Play Series, Scholastic.

Ross C. and Browne N., 1994, *Girls as Constructors in the Early Years*, Trentham Books.

Young N., 1991, *Signs of Design, The Early Years*, The Design Centre.

Catalogue: *Criteria for Play Equipment* from Community Playthings (for address see General Resources, page 151) has excellent illustrations of many kinds of wooden blocks.

Video: Bruce T., 1992, *Building a Future: Block Play and Young Children*, The Froebel Block Play Research Group.

8 Puzzles and Table-top Activities

Jigsaw puzzles are familiar to most pre-school children, and create an excellent home-school link, as children feel relaxed and safe doing jigsaws when they first start at nursery. They are essentially a solitary experience, although children may do the large floor puzzles in a small group.

Jigsaws range from very simple inset boards for the youngest children, to very intricate puzzles for adults. Sometimes children will choose easy puzzles when they are feeling the need for reassurance, and at other times will enjoy the challenge of more demanding jigsaws. They are ideal for sick children, as they can be set up on a tray for those in bed. It is important that no pieces are missing, particularly for the younger children, as this spoils the pleasure of completing a task satisfactorily.

Board games similarly come in varying degrees of difficulty. Most are not suitable for the under-4s as the children will not have yet gained the concept of taking turns, and may get upset at having to wait and spoil the game for others. Most games are a variation of Ludo or Snakes and Ladders.

Matching games, such as Picture Lotto and Connect, help children to see similarities and differences, and to match like with like. These can be played by one child alone, or with a group of children.

Card games, such as Snap, Pairs or Sevens, are enjoyed by children of 4 years upwards. Snap or Pairs cards can be made quite easily, using pictures or photographs familiar to the children's cultural background. Ask permission before introducing packs of cards into your placement, as some establishments look on cards as an introduction to gambling.

Children enjoy threading beads and cotton reels, and again these are graded in order of difficulty, the younger children finding the larger beads the easiest.

Pegboards and mosaic pieces help children to make patterns.

You might come across sewing cards, where children are asked to go in and out of holes with a lace or a threaded needle. Older children sometimes sew simple projects such as bookmarks or needle cases.

AMOUNT OF SPACE		TYPE OF SPACE	
Whole area		Outside	
Half area		Inside	■
Quarter area		Hard surface	
Small area	■	Carpeted	■
		Table space	■
TYPE OF PLAY		**INVOLVEMENT OF ADULT**	
Solitary	■	Essential	
Parallel	■	Enriching	■
Small group	■	Not always necessary	■
Large group		Can be intrusive	■

ESSENTIAL MATERIALS
Equipment named on previous page

SUGGESTED ADDITIONAL MATERIALS
None

VALUE TO AREAS OF DEVELOPMENT AND LEARNING

Physical
All table toys are a great aid to developing gross and fine manipulative skills and the acquisition of precision movements.

Social and moral
When played in groups, these toys and games involve children's turn-taking, cooperation and sharing. Games with rules aid understanding of society.

Emotional
Some games are competitive, and children have to learn to lose gracefully. Self-esteem is gained by the successful completion of puzzles.

Intellectual
Doing jigsaw puzzles and sorting and matching games helps children to find similarities and differences and so are valuable early reading activities. Card games encourage memory and quickness of thought. Concentration, logical thought, reasoning and perseverance are necessary for all these activities.

Language
Explaining and understanding instructions for games helps language development.

Aesthetic and spiritual
Jigsaws and Picture Lotto can be linked to the natural world of beauty. They can also reflect life experiences and cultural celebrations. Children will gain by sharing such knowledge.

Sensory
A tactile jigsaw is useful for a child with visual impairment.

Good Practice

- All equipment should be stored in strong boxes, where the children have access and are allowed to select their own activity. Plastic equipment should be washed regularly.
- A good range and variety of puzzles should be available, to cater for all abilities and to allow choice. If there are pieces missing, the puzzle should be discarded, unless replacement pieces can be supplied.
- Card games and matching games should be complete.
- Other table top toys should be provided in sufficient quantity to allow a group to play together.

Essential points

Equal opportunities

- Equipment reflecting cultural diversity should be bought. For example puzzles with pictures from around the world, depicting people of different ethnic origins, are available from most catalogues.
- Boys may need encouragement to sew.
- Several sets of photographic jigsaws should include children with disabilities.

Safety

- Care needs to be taken with small beads and pegs with younger children, to make sure they are not swallowed or inserted into ears and noses.
- Blunt needles are quite satisfactory for sewing Binca material or felt, and are a useful way of encouraging children to be careful when they progress to using sharper ones.

Resources

Davies J., 1989, *Children's Games*, Piatkus Books.

Taverner J., 1998, *Table Top Games*, Learning Through Play Series, Scholastic.

Jigsaws for children with special needs are available from NES Arnold (for address see General Resources, page 151)

9 | *Books and Storytelling*

Enjoyment of books and stories starts in the home. Before a child is a year old, he or she enjoys looking at pictures or photographs while being cuddled by an adult and read to. Nurturing this love of books is probably the key factor in the later aquisition of reading skills, which in turn leads to academic attainment and a lifelong pleasure in reading.

Young children in particular, derive great pleasure in being told stories. These can be personalised, either being tales from the storyteller's past, or stories where the listener becomes the centre of the tale. Sometimes props can be used, such as puppets and flannelgraphs as, apart from making the story more vivid, they also help the child's memory when re-telling the story. Flannelgraphs are pictures mounted on board. They tell the story and can be attached to a felt board one by one. They can be used with or without an adult. Some stories, such as The Great Big Enormous Turnip, lend themselves to flannelgraphs, as the story is simple and the characters are added in sequence.

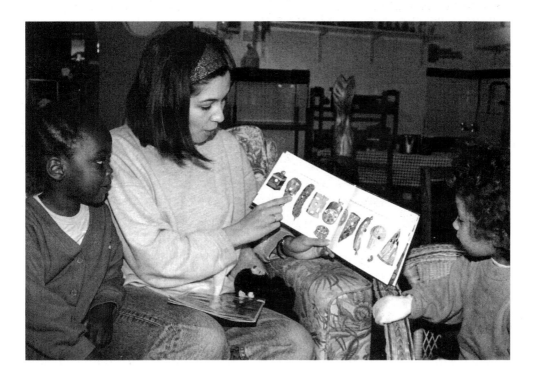

Being told or read a story is delightful and relaxing. Many parents read to their child just before settling him or her down to sleep, and sick children benefit enormously from a familiar comforting story, and the sole attention of a loved adult.

Once a child starts school around the age of 5 years, a great deal of emphasis is placed on learning to read. Nowadays, parents are encouraged to come in to schools to hear children read, and take books home to continue the good work. Children often read in pairs, hearing each other, and practising their skills.

When you are in your primary school placement, you are likely to be involved in the daily literacy hour working with children in large and small groups, concentrating on reading, writing and spelling.

As a childcare and education worker, you will sometimes be reading to one or two children from a book of their choice, and you will be able to establish a close relationship. Children can participate in turning a page, placing pictures on a flannelgraph or lifting a flap. On other occasions you will be reading to a group of children preferably all at a similar stage of development, and you will choose a book with the children where the pictures can be seen, and the story is age-appropriate. Reading to a group needs careful preparation beforehand.

Poetry for older children will enrich their vocabulary and let them know that it is acceptable to express emotions. This may encourage older children to write their own poems. For younger children humorous verse is a good introduction. Repetitive rhyming is most helpful to children with limited language skills. For all children, it can, like books, open up a world of fantasy and imagination.

AMOUNT OF SPACE		TYPE OF SPACE	
Whole area		Outside	■
Half area		Inside	■
Quarter area		Hard surface	
Small area	■	Carpeted	■
		Table space	
TYPE OF PLAY		**INVOLVEMENT OF ADULT**	
Solitary	■	Essential	
Parallel	■	Enriching	■
Small group	■	Not always necessary	■
Large group		Can be intrusive	

ESSENTIAL MATERIALS

A good range of books and stories, from picture books with no words to picture books with a very simple narrative: highly illustrated story books, bound books with a picture on every page, books with a longer narrative and some illustrations, information or resource books. There should be a balance of books that reflect a diversity of life styles, religions and cultures, and dilemmas that are faced by children, such as coping with divorce or a new baby in the family

A comfortable, well lit area for children to relax and read, and nearby storage

SUGGESTED ADDITIONAL MATERIALS

Puppets: glove, finger, string, paper, material

Props: whatever is appropriate to the story, such as dolls, stuffed toys, cars, small world toys and so on

Flannelgraphs: characters and scenes from a book or story, which are made out of felt or a similar material, and will stick to a board as the story progresses.

Access to a tape recorder

Taped sounds or percussion music to accompany a story

Taped stories which the children can listen to themselves, together with the book. Most successful when the story is taped by an adult they know, and they can hear themselves participating.

VALUE TO AREAS OF DEVELOPMENT AND LEARNING

Physical
Turning pages demands manipulative control. Sitting still enough to listen needs physical control.

Social and moral
Reading in a small group is a cooperative sharing experience. Turns have to be taken when asking questions about the story and discussing the book. Respect must be learnt for the ideas of others. Many stories help children to discriminate between right and wrong. Others show children caring for each other.

Emotional
Being able to read gives a child independence. Empathising with a character in a book allows a child to understand his or her own feelings. On a one-to-one basis, reading with an adult is a nurturing experience, giving feelings of love and security. Being able to read gives a child self-esteem and a sense of achievement. It is a home-school link.

Intellectual
Books and stories encourage concentration, extend the child's knowledge of the world and aid imagination. The ability to use information and resource material links in with all other activities. Re-telling stories helps develop memory and the ability to articulate ideas. Learning poetry and verse aids recall and memory, and often remains with you throughout life.

Language
Books offer new vocabulary and foster listening skills. Repetitive stories and verse help children with limited language.

Aesthetic and spiritual
Attractive illustrations make children aware of the beauty of the world.

Sensory
Books can be a visual delight. Some books made today have buttons to press allowing areas of the book to light up or to make a noise. Others have areas to scratch to release a smell. Many are tactile, having pages with different textures one can feel.

Good Practice

- In schools and pre-schools it is usual to have a Book Corner. This should be sited in a quiet area of the room, where there is not constant movement to and fro, in a good light, and with comfortable furniture, away from the messy or natural play area

- Books should always be available to the children and, ideally, an adult always there to read to them if required. Children enjoy reading on the floor, so it is most important that this area is carpeted and kept clean. Books should be stored on shelves at the children's height, with some displayed on a table or on a rack so that children can see the covers. They should be kept in good condition, and children taught at a young age to treat them with respect. Books need inspecting for scribbles, torn or missing pages or any other sort of damage, and should be removed if they cannot be repaired properly. Children who damage books should be encouraged to help in the repair. The display of books should be changed regularly, but favourite books should be left out as long as required. Books can be made by the children, and these are often highly valued.
- A comprehensive range of books needs to be available. The books should reflect our multicultural society, with stories from countries around the world and some books in the heritage languages of the children in the group. Great care must be taken to avoid stereotyping when choosing books, whether it is in the area of race, religion, class, age, disability or gender. Positive images reflecting

the diversity of culture and families today need to be included, together with stories portraying children with disabilities and girls in strong roles.

■ Children identify with characters in books, and you should be aware of the needs of all the children in your group in order to help them make sense of their feelings and to promote self-esteem and feelings of worth. Children of all ages need information and factual books, linking in with other areas of their work, and to extend their experiences and knowledge.

■ Remember the value of telling stories, as well as reading books. This is particularly valuable for the younger children, as the story you make up can be personalised with the names of the children in the group, and will therefore hold their interest more. Not all children like to be the centre of attention, so you need to be sensitive to this. Story telling frees the hands so that you can use props to illustrate your story, and this helps children who may not yet be fluent in English to understand and participate more.

■ For children to get the best from a group story, you need to think carefully about several things: firstly, the size of the group. Up to the age of 4, six children should be the maximum number of 2- and 3-year-olds. It is important to maintain eye contact with these young children, so as to keep their interest and participation. Generally 4-year-olds are able to concentrate in larger groups, but not all of them can do this, and you need to take the developmental age into account as well as how much experience the child has had of group stories. Secondly, the appropriateness of the book or story needs thinking about. The youngest children will be content with stories about familiar events, such as shopping and bedtime, and some simple tales that are happily resolved about other children and animals. As children's experience of stories is extended, longer books about imaginary events can be read, but always be aware of frightening the children. Young children's imagination is very vivid, and fairy stories can be terrifying, as they often deal with tales of rejection and separation. Ogres and witches should be left for an older age group, and even then not all children feel comfortable with fantasy tales, as they may still have difficulty in discriminating fact from fiction. Thirdly, the way that you read stories has a good deal of bearing on how much the children will enjoy them. Your voice should not be dull and monotonous, and you should try to cultivate different tones and pitches for dialogue. You should choose stories you enjoy reading and telling, and you will need to be familiar with the story you are going to read. If you are cajoled into reading a story you dislike, this will show in your delivery of it.

■ Timing is important. It is futile to expect children to gain a great deal from a story session if it is placed just before dinner time, when hungry children are distracted by the smell of food and interrupted by being told to go and wash their hands. To read to them just before home time, when the children are tired and falling asleep, and distracted by parents arriving to collect them is also a wasted opportunity. Children who have not really settled in to the group will not listen to a word, as they are anxiously watching the door and waiting to be collected. Far better to read stories in the middle of working sessions, when the children have no expectations of immediately seeing loved adults, and are not too tired and hungry to concentrate.

- Not all young children are ready to sit in a group, and a quiet alternative activity should be allowed until the child wants to join in. All other activities in the pre-school are voluntary, and sitting with a group for any reason should be as well.
- Children want the same stories time and time again, but occasionally you need to introduce new stories. Sometimes it is a good idea to leave the book on the display table for a little while first, so that the children can familiarise themselves with the pictures.
- Some books have many words in them that are unfamiliar to the children. It is not a good idea to change the words into more familiar ones as you go along. This is disrespectful to the writer, and it deprives the children of learning new words. If the language is so difficult that the children become bored, re-introduce the book another time with older children.
- Allow some time for relaxed discussion at the end of the story. Children do not always want to talk about the book, so do not force them to do so. Sometimes children want to participate throughout the reading or telling of the story. It depends on your personal preference as to whether you let them do this or wait until the end of the story session. Usually the youngest children cannot wait until the end if they have something to say!
- Other adults might want to be involved in story time. Sometimes parents will read to a small group of children, and this is particularly useful if you have bilingual children in your class. Reading sessions are sometimes held in your local library, or the librarian will come into the school to read to the children. Older children should be encouraged to join the library, and the younger ones should be familiar with the building.
- Books should represent the whole spectrum of society, not just the ideal nuclear family with no financial problems.
- When buying new books, or borrowing books from the library, care must be taken to make sure that none of them contain elements which could offend adults or distress children, by displaying offensive attitudes. It is equally important to be vigilant in this if the children you care for are from one ethnic group only.
- Show children that you enjoy books, as it is by your example that they will learn to value and appreciate books and stories. Remember that books have a place in most of the activities and experiences of the children, and always be ready to provide the appropriate book when the occasion demands.

Wendy Ewer has devised the checklist on pages 64–65 which may be useful when selecting books to use with children.

CHECKLIST FOR BOOKS AND STORIES

Name _____

Date _____ Age of children _____ No. of children _____

Title _____ Author _____

Publisher _____ ISBN No. _____

Type of book: Fact   Fiction   Picture book   Poetry/Rhyme

1 My choice of book/story was agreed with _____

2 I presented the book by   reading   telling   with a visual aid

3 I prepared, before sharing the book, by _____

_____

4 a) The place was suitable because _____

_____

b) The children and adults were comfortable because _____

_____

c) All the children could see because _____

d) I settled the children for the session by _____

_____

5 The story was suitable for the children's age, level of development, concentration and interest because _____

6 a) I made eye contact with the child/ren _____

_____

b) I used different voice tones and volume for _____

_____

7 I dealt with (interruptions or distractions) _____

_____

8 The children participated by _____

9 The children's comments were _____

_____

And I responded by _____

_____

10 I engaged their attention, and helped their concentration by _____

_____

11 a) I finished the session by _____

_____

b) The children reacted to the story/book by _____

_____

12 The book reflected positive images by _____

_____

13 I could use this story/book again with _____

_____

Comments _____

_____

_____

_____

_____

I verify that the candidate has read/told/shared this story/book as stated above

Signed _____

Essential points

Equal opportunities

- Books are an ideal way of presenting positive images of children from many varied ethnic groups. By giving all children insight into different cultures with their own traditional stories and into varied child-rearing practices, they will learn to value and respect people for what they are, and to challenge stereotypical attitudes. Check the illustrations for stereotypes. Make sure that children with special needs are not depicted as being weak and needy.
- There should be books in heritage languages so that all parents can read to their children in the classroom, and the value attached to this can be seen by other children.
- Girls should be depicted in strong roles, not as dependent passive onlookers.
- Books are available to help children who are having to deal with problems in their private lives, such as hospitalisation, parental separation, bereavement and so on.
- There should be more books depicting children with special needs as central characters in a story.
- Books which can be read in English and in sign language can be bought. Tactile books can be purchased or made for the visually impaired and for very young children.

Safety

Books do not present a hazard.

Resources

Agard J., 1986, *Say It Again Granny*, Magnet.

Botham J. and Elliot D., 1993, *Language and Literacy in the Early Years*, BAECE.

Emblem V. and Schmitz H., 1992, *Learning Through Story*, Bright Ideas for Early Years Series, Scholastic Publications Ltd.

Fitzsimmons J. and Whiteford R., 1994, *English Key Stage 1*, Blueprint Series, Stanley Thornes (Publishers) Ltd.

Gawith G., 1990, *Reading Alive*, A. & C. Black (Publishers) Ltd.

Hill E., *Where's Spot* and *Spot Goes to School* (both available in sign language for hearing impaired children), Baker Books.

Jame F. and Kerr A., 1993, *On First Reading*, Belair Publications.

Johnson P., 1990, *A Book of One's Own*, Hodder & Stoughton.

Magee Wes, 1992, *Poetry Compilation*, Scholastic Publications Ltd.

Morris H., 1992, *The New Where's That Poem?*, Stanley Thornes (Publishers) Ltd.

Rosen M., 1994, *A World of Poetry*, Kingfisher.

Walter C., 1989, *An Early Start to Poetry*, Macdonald Education.

Wason-Ellam L., 1987, *Sharing Stories with Children: Reading Aloud and Storytelling*, Warren West, Calgary, Alberta.

Weekes A., 1991, *My First Word Book*, Dorling Kindersley Ltd.

Weekes A., 1993, *My First Dictionary*, Dorling Kindersley Ltd.

Bookshops and Book Associations

Africa Book Centre Ltd., 38 King Street, London WC2E 8JT.

Bookspread, 58 Tooting Bec Road, London SW17 8BE. Telephone 0181 767 6377.

Working Group Against Racism in Children's Resources, Publications Dept., PO Box 3554, London N1 3RA. Guidelines and selected titles, and 100 picture books.

Letterbox Library, 2D Leroy House, 436 Essex Road, London N1 3BR. Telephone 0171 226 l633.

Society for Storytelling, 52 Normanton Lane, Keyworth, Nottinghamshire NG12 5HA.

10 *Music, Sound and Movement*

Music is a familiar part of everybody's life. Some people think that foetuses respond to music in their mother's womb. It seems to have a calming effect and is even attributed to linking neurons in the brain, promoting intelligence.

From a very young age, babies will respond without discrimination but with enjoyment to a wide range of musical and rhythmic sounds. Lullabies are often used to soothe babies to sleep. As children grow older, their musical taste is formed by outside influences, particularly those of the family, the culture they are born into, the media, and their primary carers and peers.

It seems entirely natural to move in response to rhythm, and moving to music and dancing is enjoyed throughout life, by children and adults within all cultures.

Experimenting with musical instruments and singing helps children discriminate sounds and aids their language development. In some classrooms and homes, singing or rhyming is quite natural, and carries on between the children and adults as a way of normal communication.

AMOUNT OF SPACE		TYPE OF SPACE	
Whole area	■	Outside	■
Half area	■	Inside	■
Quarter area	■	Hard surface	■
Small area		Carpeted	■
		Table space	
TYPE OF PLAY		**INVOLVEMENT OF ADULT**	
Solitary		Essential	
Parallel		Enriching	■
Small group	■	Not always necessary	■
Large group	■	Can be intrusive	■

ESSENTIAL EQUIPMENT
Repertoire of songs and rhymes, and the confidence to sing them
Space for movement

SUGGESTED ADDITIONAL EQUIPMENT

Record, CD or cassette player

Range of records, compact discs and cassette tapes, containing music and sounds from around the world

Tape recorder

A range of good quality percussion instruments, such as shakers, Chinese wood claps, Indian dancer's bells, and steel drums

Stringed instrument played by a member of staff

Instruments made by the children

Simple wind instruments, such as Indian pipes and Irish penny whistles

Resource books

Good Practice

■ Music should always be available to children. A music table set up with a selection of good quality instruments and those made by the children should stand in an accessible area of the room. Instruments should be changed regularly, in the same way as books in the book corner. Children need to be shown how to treat instruments with respect, but if any are damaged they should be removed for repair. The youngest children have the keenest hearing and therefore should always have access to the best instruments that can be provided.

VALUE TO AREAS OF DEVELOPMENT AND LEARNING

Physical
Moving to music and using instruments develops body and spatial awareness, balance, coordination and agility. Playing instruments and executing finger rhymes helps develop fine manipulative skills and hand-eye coordination.

Social and moral
Music is an opportunity to share experiences and to provide an introduction to music from diverse cultures. It is a non-competitive activity, and helps build relationships. Children have to learn to share and take turns, and to have consideration for others.

Emotional
Music encourages freedom of expression, and the release of emotions such as pleasure, fear, and frustration. It can be relaxing and therapeutic, and can raise self-esteem and confidence, especially in older children when performing.

Intellectual
Music aids memory, imagination, concentration, sequencing, classification, creativity and discrimination.

Language
Singing develops expressive language, articulation, vocabulary, diction and expressive use of the voice. Music develops listening skills and heightens a feeling for language.

Aesthetic and spiritual
Music and songs from all cultures will help children to develop positive feelings of acceptance and a sense of belonging and encourages respect. Music can be an aesthetic and spiritual experience and is often uplifting.

Sensory
Hearing is sharpened by the practice of discriminating sounds. Touch is stimulated by handling well-made instruments.

Occasionally there should be a time when the children can listen to some music which they might not otherwise come across, such as music from different parts of the world, electronic sound patterns, operatic arias, rap or modern jazz. Apart from being a relaxing experience, it extends the children's musical appreciation and knowledge.

■ There should be music sessions at least once a day. These should be very short for the youngest children – ten minutes is quite enough. They do not have to be directed by a music specialist and all that is required of you in organising the session is a constantly up-dated repertoire of suitable songs and rhymes, and the confidence to lead the session in a lively and enthusiastic manner. Although it will distance you from the children, it adds a great deal to the musicality of the session if you are able to play an instrument, such as a guitar or the piano. These instruments will leave your voice free for singing, but if this talent is not available a record or a tape will do almost as well. You should offer familiar songs and activities as well as introducing new ones. Actions and movements designed to go with songs and rhymes help children concentrate, offer enjoyment and motivation, and help them to interpret music with their bodies.

■ At certain times during the day, when the noise will not interfere with other quieter activities, children should be encouraged to experiment with the instruments available in making their own music. The adult should be on hand to help them with this improvisation.

■ Not all music sessions require instruments. Just singing songs that appeal to children is an enjoyable and worthwhile experience. Sometimes children might have access to a large space such as the school hall, and moving to rhythmic patterns that can be clapped by hand or beaten out on a percussion instrument helps children to move in a controlled way. On other occasions, some loud music to dance to will allow self-expression and release of tension, in vigorous physical exercise.

■ Remember not to have music playing constantly in the background. This will deaden children's discrimination.

Activity

Plan a music or a movement activity for **a)** 3-year-olds and **b)** 7-year-olds. How will the approach, the equipment and the adult's role vary?

Essential points

Equal opportunities

■ Be aware of gender and racial stereotypes in songs and rhymes. It is probably better to discard such songs, rather than alter the words. Take children to see local cultural festivals, with performances by dancers or musicians, as well as indigenous performers and festivals.

■ Music allows children who do not speak English to join in and participate as music is international. This aids speech and language development.

■ Every culture has its own musical traditions and instruments, such as the flute in Irish music and the steel drums in African-Caribbean rhythms. Children should be introduced to a wide variety of musical traditions.

■ Use songs and records or tapes in various languages, and in different musical styles. Ask parents and staff to teach the children the songs they grew up with, remembering there are various different European cultures too. Collect musical instruments from various cultures.

■ Children with disabilities will find simple, repetitive songs and rhymes relaxing and soothing. All children enjoy playing percussion instruments, and special grip pads and stands are available. Children with hearing impairments enjoy listening to the vibrations of low pitched sounds. Visually impaired children need highly developed hearing skills to compensate for poor vision. Movement to music on a one-to-one basis can be particularly useful for children with multiple disabilities.

Safety

- Very young children need careful supervision, particularly when playing with homemade instruments.
- Very loud music played constantly can damage hearing.

Resources

Addison R., 1987, *Music*, Bright Ideas for Early Years Series, Scholastic Publications Ltd.

Danes E., 1993, *First Book of Music*, Usborne Publishing.

Drew H., 1993, *My First Music Book*, Dorling Kindersley Ltd.

East H. (compiler), 1989, *The Singing Sack*, Songs and Stories From Around the World, A. & C. Black (Publishers) Ltd.

Evans D., 1978, *Sharing Sounds*, Longman.

Evans D. and Williams C., 1993, *Let's Explore Science*; *Sound and Music*, Dorling Kindersley Ltd.

Farrimond R. and Such L., 1977, *Seeing and Doing*, Thames Television.

Gadsby D. and Harrop B., 1979, *Ta-ra-ra boom-de-ay*, A. & C. Black (Publishers) Ltd.

Harrison K., 1986, *Look, Look, What I Can Do!*, Creative Action Ideas for Under Sevens, BBC Books.

Harrison L., 1996, *Dance and Drama*, Learning Through Play Series, Scholastic.

Harrop B., Friend L. and Gadsby D., 1995, *Okki-tokki-unga*, A. & C. Black (Publishers) Ltd.

McKellar S., 1993, *Counting Rhymes*, Dorling Kindersley Ltd.

Matterson E., 1991, *This Little Puffin*, Puffin Books.

Merry K., *The Big Big Multicultural Music Book* (and tape), available from Letterbox Library (for address see Bookshops and Book Associations, page 67)

Mort L. and Morris J., 1991, *Starting with Rhyme*, Bright Ideas for Early Years Series, Scholastic Publications Ltd.

Opie I. and P., 1963, *The Puffin Book of Nursery Rhymes*, Puffin Books.

Pegg L., 1998, *Music*, Learning Through Play Series, Scholastic.

Taylor D., 1994, *Action Rhymes*, Ladybird Books.

Ware M., 1987, *Time to Dance*, Belair Publications.

Whiteford R., 1991, *Music and Movement*, Bright Ideas for Early Years Series, Scholastic Publications Ltd.

Wilkes A., 1992, *Animal Nursery Rhymes*, Dorling Kindersley Ltd.

Music Through Play, Learn Through Play Series, PPA
Songs, Games and Stories from Around the World, 1990, UNICEF UK.

Catalogue: Acorn percussion, Unit 34, Abbey Business Centre, Ingate Place, London SW8 3NS. Telephone 0171 627 3020.

11 *Outside Play*

Nearly every activity that takes place in the classroom or nursery can equally well be taken outside if the weather permits. Some activities can take place only outside, and it is to these that this chapter refers.

A safe outside play area is vital for young children, to exercise and let off steam, to practise their developing physical skills and to build self-confidence. Some children have limited access to safe outdoor play and need fresh air and exercise to promote good health.

A safe outdoor play area allows children freedom to investigate and explore their environment with little adult restriction. It should be an integral part of the pre-school provision and, ideally, children should have access to it at all times. This should be taken into account when planning activities, always remembering that outside play should not be compulsory, any more than any other activity. Very young children, who are not used to playing outside, may find the playground intimidating and overwhelming at first, but when their self-confidence has developed will soon enjoy being outside if allowed to choose for themselves.

Activity

Give some reasons why many children do not always have the opportunity to play outside freely when they are not at school or nursery.

In an outside play area attached to a pre-school establishment or a school, ideally, there should be space and storage for wheeled toys, a grass area, an area for gardening, some trees and bushes to give shelter and privacy, and a surface suitable for the securing of climbing equipment and slides.

The playground must be effectively supervised and safety aspects taken into account. What is provided will influence the quality of the play. The presence of an enthusiastic adult who joins in the children's play, rather than just standing outside with a cup of tea, will ensure maximum enjoyment and promotion of development. Traditional games may be organised, either by the children, or by an adult, such as 'What's the Time, Mr Wolf?', Hide and Seek, and Ring-O'-Roses. Obviously, children should not be pressurised into taking part if they do not wish to.

AMOUNT OF SPACE		TYPE OF SPACE	
Whole area	■	Outside	■
Half area		Inside	
Quarter area		Hard surface	
Small area		Carpeted	
		Table space	

TYPE OF PLAY		INVOLVEMENT OF ADULT	
Solitary	■	Essential	
Parallel	■	Enriching	■
Small group	■	Not always necessary	■
Large group	■	Can be intrusive	

ESSENTIAL EQUIPMENT

Outside area

Storage facility

Protective and warm clothing, such as spare wellingtons, gloves and hats; sun
   hats and sun block

SUGGESTED ADDITIONAL EQUIPMENT

Large equipment, which might include a climbing frame, planks, galvanised
   metal A-frames, barrels, and a slide

Large covered containers for natural materials, such as sand and water

Benches for sitting on

Large cardboard cartons; wooden and plastic crates; tyres; tree trunks; cubes
   with holes

Trampolines; ladders; tunnels; drainpipes, plastic guttering, pieces of
   hosepipe

Pails and large brushes for 'painting' paving stones and walls

Patch of ground for the cultivation of flowers and quick growing vegetables;
   gardening equipment such as trowels and small forks, watering cans, flower
   pots; bird table

Place reserved for making mud pies

Bicycles, scooters and other wheeled toys, which can be used by more than one
   child, such as haycarts, porter's trolleys, pushchairs and articulated push-
   alongs

Small equipment such as pulleys, ropes, decorators' buckets with large paint
   brushes, quoits, bats, balls and beanbags, blankets and magnifying glasses

It is fun to use chalk outside, but some placements feel it may lead to children
   writing graffiti

VALUE TO AREAS OF DEVELOPMENT AND LEARNING

Physical
Playing outside releases surplus energy and is a licence to make more noise. It stimulates the appetite, aids digestion and circulation, promotes sleep, and gives resistance to infection and a healthy skin, as well as developing muscle tone, manipulative skills, balance and control. Children develop skills, such as stopping and starting, running, hopping, digging, planting, skipping, climbing, pedalling, swinging, steering, crawling through and under equipment and carrying.

Social and moral
Children share, take turns and collaborate, take responsibility for sharing space, and gain understanding of the rules governing outside play and games. They learn respect for living things.

Emotional
Outside play is enjoyable, releasing tension and aggression. It gives freedom from restriction. Challenging play leads to self-confidence and self-esteem and gives children power over the environment. It allows some children to succeed who may fail in the classroom.

Intellectual
Outside play encourages concentration and alertness and stimulates intellectual curiosity and powers of observation. It helps children to understand concepts of height, width, speed, distance, growth and spatial relationships. Children can be given some responsibility for planning and decision making.

Language
Outside play develops the use and understanding of spatial terms. Children learn the 'language of the playground', including traditional playground rhymes.

Aesthetic and spiritual
Children learn to observe the wonders of nature, such as rainbows, reflections in puddles, birds, animals and insects, growing plants and changing seasons.

Sensory
The outside area provides a stimulus for all the senses and an opportunity for a range of imaginary play experiences.

Good Practice

- The successful outside play area needs careful planning, so that the children can play as freely as possible without being run over by wheeled toys or hit on the head by footballs. The equipment should be linked to the ages and stages of the children, so that the younger children are not put at risk, but there is challenging equipment for the older ones. If the age range is very wide, you may need to have separate areas for the babies and for the older children.
- Children should help to plan the outside play, by taking turns to choose the equipment, and should also help set it out and put it away. There should be a breadth and a balance in the outdoor curriculum, taking into account the needs of all the children, the older ones needing more complex play, such as assault courses, and the newcomers able to try out new skills without interference.
- Inside and outside play should be freely available, and neither area should be compulsory in the pre-school.
- Toys which can be used only by one child at a time, such as bicycles, can cause more trouble than they are worth. Seen as representing power, children are often reluctant to share, and quarrels ensue over whose turn it is and how long someone has been on the bike. On the other hand, they give the opportunity of acquiring skills such as balance, steering and pedalling, not available to some children.
- Adults should enjoy and be involved in outside play, not just passively supervising. The area needs to be kept clean, and all equipment washed and serviced regularly.
- Children must be dressed according to the weather, protected against the sun as well as the rain.
- There is a need for resource books, so that amateur gardeners, ecologists and scientists can have their questions answered.
- Parents must be informed of any accidents, and details recorded in the Accident Book.

Activity

List different types of outdoor play, and give examples of equipment that could be used to extend each type.

Essential points

Equal opportunities

- It has been observed that boys tend to dominate outside play and the use of the equipment. Measures can be taken to redress the balance by, for example, allowing only the girls to use the wheeled toys for one session, or see that they have access first.

- Guard against having expectations of children's physical abilities based on stereotypes.
- Parents could be asked for suggestions for games from all cultures, to reflect diversity.
- For children with disabilities, soft play equipment such as foam-filled large blocks, is available. Games should generally be non-competitive although some individual children might enjoy an element of competition. Plastic bats and a variety of balls can be used. Bean bags are easier to control than bouncing balls.
- Velcro straps can be fitted to bicycle pedals and some climbing equipment can be adapted, perhaps with bars across.
- Visually impaired children see white balls more clearly than coloured ones.

Safety

- Potentially, this is a very dangerous area, and children must have the rules of safety carefully explained and demonstrated to them. This needs constant reinforcing. You need to remember, if supervising hearing impaired children, that they will not hear shouted warnings.
- Check the outside area for broken glass, undesirable objects and dog mess before allowing children to play. Check all large equipment routinely, for splinters and stability, and make sure that all the joints, nuts and screws are correctly in place. If faulty, take the piece of equipment out of use and report it immediately.
- Ensure that the equipment is serviced regularly by, for example, polishing and oiling. All new equipment must be fixed securely, must meet health and safety standards and must be purchased from a recognised reputable firm.
- The area under any climbing equipment should be soft and durable, using bark chippings or rubberised tiles.
- Access to the slide should be only by the stairs, and children should come down feet first, not head first.
- Climbing equipment should never be used when wet, and needs drying well after rain before using again. This sort of equipment needs constant supervision and alertness on your part. Children should not be allowed to climb in clothes that trail behind them, in tight jeans that restrict movement or in unsuitable shoes such as those in the dressing-up box, rubber sandals or flip flops.
- There should be as few rules as possible, but these must be strictly adhered to by both children and adults.
- Assault courses are fun and challenging for children, but also need close supervision.

- Sand pits need to be kept covered when not in use so that animals cannot get in. Sand must be swept up when spilt and sieved and washed before putting back.
- Seesaws and rocking boats should be in a safe place and not rock into a wall or the sand pit. Care must be taken to see that hands do not get trapped underneath.
- Swings are dangerous unless carefully supervised and in an area with a fence around.
- The whole of the playground should be visible to the adult. The boundary wall should be high enough to discourage children climbing on it, and to prevent access to strangers. Gates and doors should be kept locked.
- Bins for rubbish should be kept in a separate place.

Resources

Bilton H., 1998, *Outdoor Play in the Early Years*, David Fulton.

Davies J., 1989, *Children's Games*, Piatkus Books.

Davis K. and Oldfield W., 1994, *Rain*; *Snow and Ice*; *Sun*; and *Wind*, See For Yourself Series, A. & C. Black (Publishers) Ltd.

De Boo M., 1992, *Action Rhymes and Games*, Bright Ideas for Early Years Series, Scholastic Publications Ltd.

Eustace V. and Heald C., 1992, *Outdoor Play*, Bright Ideas for Early Years Series, Scholastic Publications Ltd.

Filer J., 1998, *Outdoor Play*, Learning Through Play Series, Scholastic.

Heddle R. and Shipton P., 1993, *Science with Weather*, Science Activities Series, Usborne Publishing.

Heseltine P. and Holborn J., 1987, *Playgrounds: the Planning, Design and Construction of Play Environments*, Mitchell Publishing Co.

Opie I. and Opie O., 1969, *Children's Games in Street and Playground*, OUP.

Readman J., 1993, *Muck and Magic*, Search Press with the Henry Doubleday Research Association.

Sutcliffe M., 1993, *Physical Education Activities* and *Outdoor Play*, Bright Ideas for Early Years Series, Scholastic Publications Ltd.

Unwin M., 1992, *Science with Plants*, Science Activities Series Usborne Publishing.

Wetton P., 1987, *Games for PE*, Bright Ideas for Early Years Series, Scholastic Publications Ltd.

Wilkes A., 1992, *My First Garden Book*, Dorling Kindersley Ltd.

Catalogue: *Criteria for Play Equipment*, Community Playthings (for address see General Resources, page 151)

12 *Outings*

Children you are working with will have a wide variety of different experiences, and this will include their knowledge of the outside world. Some children are quite familiar with airports and holidays abroad, some may be lucky enough to enjoy different weekly outings with their family, but others may come from families where there is no money for the extra luxuries of transport and admission charges and the adults have little energy to take their children to new situations and enjoy new experiences with them.

Outings are important as a means of widening the children's environment and making them aware of other people's roles and the structure of the community in which they live. However broad their experience, children do not often have the opportunity to go for a walk at their own pace, to have questions patiently answered, and to respond to questions put to them.

In the pre-school setting, it is not necessary to be too ambitious. A walk to the park to feed the birds, to the letterbox to post a letter (and await its arrival at the nursery the next day), to the supermarket to shop for cooking ingredients or to the station to watch the trains arrive and leave are all enriching experiences.

As children progress through the infant school, outings can become more structured, and can include a visit to a swimming pool, a local farm, a zoo, a building site, the market place in the local community and a concert in church halls. In London, The Tate Gallery is quite suitable for 5-year-olds to give them their first exposure to modern art, and the Science Museum has a sensory area for young children. By 7 or 8 most children are ready for visits to all museums and art galleries, as long as the outing is kept quite short, and just one particular display is targeted.

Some schools and day care centres may take all the children, staff and parents on a grand annual outing to the seaside or a theme park. Whilst very good for staff–parent relationships, it is difficult to give the children the same individual attention as you would try to do on a less ambitious outing.

Outings are a useful way to introduce a theme or project to a class of 5-, 6-, or 7-year-olds to link with the National Curriculum.

AMOUNT OF SPACE	TYPE OF SPACE	
Whole area	Outside	■
Half area	Inside	
Quarter area	Hard surface	
Small area	Carpeted	
	Table space	

TYPE OF PLAY		INVOLVEMENT OF ADULT	
Solitary		Essential	■
Parallel		Enriching	■
Small group	■	Not always necessary	
Large group	■	Can be intrusive	

ESSENTIAL EQUIPMENT

First aid equipment
Form of identification
Appropriate clothing and sensible shoes
Tissues
Written permission from parents/carers
Money

SUGGESTED ADDITIONAL EQUIPMENT

A bag for collecting 'treasures' (if going on a nature walk)
Small games equipment (if going to the park)
Swimming costumes and towels (if going swimming)
Paper and pens (if going to museum or art gallery)
Lunch – if going to be out for the day
Spare clothing in case of accidents
Emergency money: mobile phone

Good Practice

- The younger the children, the simpler the outing, the shorter the journey, the smaller the number of children, and the greater ratio of adults to children are good rules to remember. Young children of 2 and 3 do not enjoy being in confined areas such as museums and theatres, and have the rest of their lives to enjoy them.
- Some visits have very little educational value. For example, what is a visit to a store's grotto to see Father Christmas teaching the children? That it is quite all right to sit on an old man's knee and ask for presents? Outings like this please adults. They are the ones who don't mind sitting for two hours in a coach to see the lights in a London street, whereas the children will probably have fallen asleep before getting there, and have a very limited view of the lights at best. Outings like these are all right for parents/carers to take their own child, but totally unsuitable for group outings.
- Before the outing:
  - Discuss where you are thinking of going with the team and Head of the establishment.
  - If possible, before making arrangements, visit the venue to check on opening times, safety, travel routes and facilities, such as lavatories and refreshment areas. If you are accompanied by a child or an adult in a wheelchair, you will need to check for wheelchair accessibility.
  - Discuss with a person in charge of the venue the forthcoming visit. Do they have an educational department? If possible, get hold of some literature. Check that the insurance of the establishment covers the particular outing you have in mind. For example, travelling in private transport may need special insurance cover.
  - Inform the parents/carers, and ask them to sign consent forms. Display notices with information about the outing around the school or nursery, giving departure and return times, funding for the trip, and general information. If lunch is to be provided by the parents, involve them in planning a suitable picnic lunch.
  - If any parent is unable to make a contribution to the cost of the trip, the school/nursery fund will often help by paying for the child to go. This must be done in strict confidence.

VALUE TO AREAS OF DEVELOPMENT AND LEARNING

Physical
Outings provide opportunities for fresh air and exercise, as in outside play. Walking strengthens leg muscles. Swimming tones up the whole body, and is an introduction to a form of exercise that will give pleasure throughout life.

Social and moral
Outings are a great social experience, going somewhere together as a group, with children, staff and parents involved. They provide opportunities for children to talk and relate to many children, and may lead to new friendships.There are many safety rules which have to be learnt and understood when going out together. Everyone has to behave responsibly.

Emotional
Outings are fun, and can offer a release from the humdrum existence of school. They give children confidence and self-esteem.

Intellectual
Outings offer knowledge of the outside world, and usually lead to much follow up work being carried out, in all areas of the curriculum. Children sometimes take part in the planning, and are exposed to new places, ideas and experiences.

Language
Outings offer opportunities for discussion, questions, conversations, and new vocabulary.

Aesthetic and spiritual
Some outings, such as nature walks and visits to art galleries, raise aesthetic and spiritual awareness, and inspire creativity in the children.

Sensory
This will vary from outing to outing. For example, the sense of smell will be greatly stimulated by a visit to the baker's – or the local farm! Sometimes visits can be especially chosen to stimulate children with a sensory impairment, for example a visit to a children's zoo would allow them to touch, hear, see and smell the animals.

- Make sure you have enough adults to enforce the rules of safety: for example, you should have one adult for every two pre-school children, and one adult for every four infant school children. Volunteering adults may need some clear guidelines on how to deal with difficult or challenging behaviour.
- Prepare children for the outing. Show them leaflets and posters if possible, and read them stories. Talk to them about what they are going to see and do, and stress the safety rules.

■ On the day:
- Check the travel facilities.
- Make sure you have your first aid kit, any essential medication, spare clothing, spare food for lunch (in case anyone has left theirs behind), equipment for the day, towels and tissues in case of accidents, emergency money, and if available, a mobile phone. A camera could be taken to be shared by the older children.
- Remember that the children will need close supervision at all times.
- For younger children, a badge or label should be secured on their clothing, giving the name and telephone number of the nursery, and not the name of the child, or any address. Safety rules need to be repeated at the start of the outing.
- Encourage the children to participate, explore and observe and, where appropriate, to collect items. Your enthusiasm will encourage the children to enjoy themselves. Worksheets should be provided for 6- to 7-year-olds, where the outing is part of work within the National Curriculum.

- Any children likely to be over-exuberant or anxious should be looked after by a member of staff, not someone who is not familiar with them. All children have needs, and the adults looking after the children should be sensitive to this.
   - Children should not carry a lot of money or bring anything personal which would cause distress if it was lost.
- After the outing:
   - The older children should be asked to record their experiences in some way, and while younger children might volunteer to express their pleasure in the outing in a drawing, this should not be expected.
   - The follow-up work may include, after some discussion, a variety of artwork, writing stories, poems or factual accounts, making a display, providing objects for an interest table, and a book of photographs. Younger children may begin to incorporate some of the experiences into their role play.

Activity

Plan an outing for a group of 7-year-olds which will give them an insight into a culture other than their own.

Essential points

Equal opportunities

- Outings offer opportunities to visit places of worship of many religions, a variety of shops and markets selling food from around the world, museums displaying artefacts from many places, art galleries showing art from many cultures, and to join in local celebrations and festivals which may offer an insight into our diverse society.
- Outings may offer an opportunity for children to be looked after by a person from another culture or ethnic group.
- Not all outings are gender-free, but children should be encouraged to enjoy a wide variety of experiences and opportunities.
- If you have children with special needs in your group, they will benefit greatly from an outing, so you must make sure that there is proper access, and comfortable travel arrangements. They may need more help and support, and require the sole attention of one adult.

Safety

- Before the outing, check the area for potential hazards and discard the venue you have thought of if there are too many risks to the children. If going somewhere vast, such as the seaside, delineate the boundaries within which the children are allowed to roam.
- Always be sure of having sufficient adults to look after the children safely. Make sure they are aware of their responsibilities.
- Children should hold hands when crossing a road or walking along a busy street. They should be forcefully informed of the dangers of wandering off, and the adults need to be constantly alert, counting the children and checking that no one has got momentarily left behind.
- Children need to be informed of what to do if they should get lost, and have knowledge of a pre-determined meeting place, which should be written down for younger children.
- Lunch packs should not include any bottled drinks, as these can break and become a hazard.
- Ideally, at least one of the adults should have a first aid certificate. Children needing medication on occasion, such as those with asthma, should be carefully supervised, and the medication carried by an adult.
- Ideally, all children should be transported, wearing seat belts. When exiting from any form of transport, children should alight on to the pavement, not the road.
- Children should never be left unsupervised when eating, or playing near water.
- Children should be warned never to touch or eat anything found growing.

Resources

Bryant-Mole K., 1985, *Flowers*; *Insects*; *Soil*; *Trees*, See For Yourself Series, A. & C. Black (Publishers) Ltd.

Godfrey S., 1992, *Environmental Activities*, Bright Ideas for Early Years Series, Scholastic Publications Ltd.

Heald G., 1996, *Journeys*, Themes for Early Years Series, Scholastic.

Wade W. and Hughes C., 1994, *Inspiration for Environmental Education*, Scholastic Publications Ltd.

Dorling Kindersley, Eyewitness Explorers Series: *Birds, Seashore, Shells, Trees* etc.

Usborne, First Nature Series: *Birds, Butterflies and Moths, Creepy Crawlies, Flowers, Trees*, etc.

Community Transport Association, Highbank, Halton Street, Hyde, Cheshire SK14 2NY. Telephone 0161 366 6685.

London Tourist Information Board. Telephone 0839 123 404 or 0839 123 424.

The Royal Society for Nature Conservation, The Green, Nettleham, Lincoln LN2 2NR.

13 *Displays and Interest Tables*

Displays can be on the walls, on tables, on display screens, on low chests and cupboards, done by adults, done by children or be a joint effort. It is usually quite easy to see which ones are which, and one needs to have clear aims for the displays and what they are for.

Displays can be a mixture of children's two dimensional and three dimensional work, objects, resource books, posters, materials and reproductions of famous pictures, or they can focus on just one of the above. They should be educational and child-centred, not merely decorative. They need to observed, discussed, and changed frequently. Children need the opportunity to examine and touch the displays, and they should therefore always be accessible, and at the children's level.

Displays and interest tables which revolve around a theme, help children understand their environment, and are particularly useful if they relate to an outing, which is in itself part of the curriculum. For example, a visit to the park, where leaves, pieces of wood , feathers, nuts, conkers and other natural items are collected and displayed, help children to remember the outing, to examine the material more closely, to discuss with adults what they have observed, and directs them to resource books to look up names and discover more.

Children should be involved in choosing, mounting and displaying the work.

ESSENTIAL MATERIALS
Wall space at a suitable level and table tops
Suitable mounting materials and tools for wall displays, and some material for covering the tables

PRACTICAL TIPS FOR WALL DISPLAYS
If time permits, pictures look better if they are mounted. Choose a colour that complements or contrasts with the work. Light mounts make the work look darker, and dark mounts make the work look lighter, so you need to try out different ones before reaching a decision. ·
The colour of the display boards can be changed by using backing paper.
If labelling is required, the writing should be done in lower case, with a capital letter at the beginning. The writing should be clear and well formed, and the chart on page 89 may help you with this task.

a b c d e f g h i j k l m

n o p q r s t u v w x y z

A B C D E F G H I J K

L M N O P Q R S T U

V W X Y Z

Good Practice

- All children's creative work should be treated with respect, and nothing should be displayed without asking the child's permission.
- All work is valuable, and all children should have their work displayed at some time or other, not just the most artistically talented.
- Displays are mainly for helping the children's learning, and need changing as soon as the children start to ignore them.
- Children should be allowed and encouraged to handle objects on an interest table, and the adults available to discuss any questions or comments they may have. Good displays will stimulate and inspire discussion.
- The most successful displays and interest tables are those in which the children have participated the most.
- Children's work should never be cut just to suit the display, but torn paper will need trimming.
- When the display is ready to put up, kneel on the floor so that you can see how it will look from the child's level.
- The room should always be bright, clean and colourful, so never leave up torn and tatty displays.

VALUE TO AREAS OF DEVELOPMENT AND LEARNING

Physical
Children need all their gross physical skills, stretching, reaching, balancing, bending, as well as fine skills in gluing, cutting, and placing when helping adults display their work.

Social and moral
Displays encourage interaction between children and adults, and shows them how to respect and care for others' work, to share ideas, to cooperate and to follow safety rules.

Emotional
Displays foster a sense of achievement and self-esteem. Some displays help children with their feelings, for example jealousy of a new baby.

Intellectual
Displays encourage mathematical skills, such as measurement, spatial awareness, patterns and shapes. They encourage children to think, ask questions, solve problems and make decisions. They stimulate memory recall.

Language
Displays encourage discussion and stimulate listening skills.

Aesthetic and spiritual
Displays help children to become aware of their environment and are pleasing to the eye. They help to make the room a happy and comfortable place. Can be linked to spiritual awareness, through a sense of awe and wonder.

Sensory
Displays offer children the opportunity to explore and handle different materials and textures and should be a visual delight. Displays can be designed to stimulate a particular sense, such as smell or taste.

Activity

Set up an interest table for the children.
1 Did it stimulate discussion?
2 Did it convey information to parents and visitors?
3 What did you learn from this display?

Essential points

Equal opportunities

■ Make sure that all the children have the opportunity to display their work or to contribute items.

■ Displays offer an opportunity to look at our multicultural diversity, and for all the children and their parents to take part.

Safety

■ It is important that all children participate in displaying work, but obviously very sharp scissors, Stanley knives, glue and staple guns should be handled only by adults, and not left lying around.

■ Displays should not be hung from the ceiling, placed near fire exits, cover fire regulations or other safety signs, placed over light switches, near alarm sensors, or have glitter on them that might fall into the eyes.

■ Objects chosen for an interest table need to be safe when handled. For example, there should not be anything too small which might be inserted into an ear or nose, or choke a small child. Glass objects might break and wooden ones splinter, heavy ones could be thrown or dropped on a toe. Sharp objects could cut and fragile ones break.

■ If displaying food, it should be fresh and changed regularly.

■ Paper is a fire hazard, and some walls might not be suitable for display.

Resources

Booth W., Briten P. and Scott F., 1987, *Themes Familiar*, Belair Publications.

Cooper H. et al, 1996, *Display in the Classroom*, David Fulton.

Edwards J., March 1992, 'Shown to Advantage', in *Child Education*.

Makoff J. and Duncan L., 1986, *Display for All Seasons*, Belair Publications.

There are a great many religious and cultural festivals to celebrate, from all over the world, and quite a few have become a part of all our lives, particularly those of our young children.

Religious and cultural festivals

Autumn term	Spring term	Summer term
Harvest Festival	Rastafarian Christmas	May Day
Rosh Hashana (Jewish New Year)	Chinese New Year	Dragon Boat Festival
Yom Kippur (Day of Atonement)	Shrove Tuesday	Carnival
	Ash Wednesday	Raksha Bandhan (Festival of Sisters)
Sukkot (Jewish Harvest Festival)	Mothering Sunday	Father's Day
	Passover	
Ethiopian New Year (Rastafarian)	Ramadan	American Independence Day
All Souls Day	St Patrick's Day	Wesak
Divali (Festival of Light)	St David's Day	Pentacost
Guy Fawkes	St George's Day	Whitsuntide
Remembrance Sunday	Lent	Festival of Hungry Ghosts (Chinese)
Thanksgiving	Easter	
St Andrew's Day	Eid-ul Fitr	Birthday of Haile Selassie
Birthday of Guru Nanak Dev Ji (Sikh)	Saraswati Puja	Birthday of Muhammad
	Holi (Festival of Colour)	
Chanukah (Jewish Festival of Light)	Baisakhi	Janamashtami
	Martin Luther King Day	Shavuot
Advent	Lantern Festival (Chinese)	World Environment Day
Christmas		
Kwanzaa	April Fool's Day	Raksha Bandhan

It is important, because of our diverse multiracial society, to know about festivals celebrated by all the ethnic and religious groups in the country, as well as the dominant Christian ones of Christmas and Easter and events such as Guy Fawkes celebrations. Because of this added richness, all our children will grow up with knowledge and respect for all cultures.

It is vital for children from all groups to feel that their culture and religion is respected and acknowledged by their peers. Groups of children from just one culture should also have the opportunity to explore other cultures and understand that we live in a multicultural society, far richer than they might have realised.

Sometimes parents are not involved in advising and organising festival celebrations, and this can lead to misinformation and may even upset some parents.

Primary schools and nurseries use festivals as themes from which children learn. The example shown on page 94 uses Divali, The Festival of Light, as its central theme.

ESSENTIAL EQUIPMENT

It is not worthwhile celebrating any festival without having either a good supply of or access to relevant information, clothes, music, food, artefacts, and books.

A Mehndi hand pattern

Social and moral
Celebrate the festival together.
Make a rangoli, cook together – learn to share and cooperate.
Hear the story of the victory of good over evil.
Discuss making new beginnings.

Language
Make a 'take home' book with the children to discuss with parents.
Learn songs and rhymes.
Tell the story and discuss.
Write in Gujarati and Bengali. Listen to tapes in several languages.
Write Divali cards.

Music and movement
Listen and dance to Indian music.
Play appropriate instruments.

Art and craft/Aesthetic appreciation
Make big rangoli patterns for display.
Make Divali cards, using small rangoli patterns to take home.
Portray the story in 3D.
Block print rangoli patterns.
Make divas from plasticine or clay.
Make mehndi pattern on hands.
Make paper chains and hanging garlands.
Make candles.
Make shadow puppets.

Mathematics
Make shapes and patterns.
Sequence the Divali story.
Discuss time past, present and tomorrow.

DIVALI

Science and technology
Observe changes that occur in cooking (onion bhaja, chapatti, sweets, biscuits, vegetables).
Observe effect of oxygen on burning. Observe light and dark; and light and shadow.
Make a lighthouse.

Environmental studies
Possible visit to a temple.
Provision of appropriate dressing-up clothes.
Hold a Sari day.
Relevent utensils and equipment in the Home Corner.

Sensory
The smell and taste of food.
The smell of incense sticks.
Awareness of light and dark.

VALUE TO AREAS OF DEVELOPMENT AND LEARNING

Physical
Festivals encourage children to dance and to play instruments, thereby using large muscles, and use fine manipulative skills in the making of masks, clothes, art and craft work and cooking.

Social and moral
Festivals are a large social event, with the whole group working and planning together. Learning about cultures and religions other than one's own teaches respect. Understanding and asking questions about the moral codes of religions helps children to understand and develop their own ethical code.

Emotional
Celebrating festivals gives all the children a feeling of identity and self-esteem. It sometimes releases tension in its exuberance.

Intellectual
All areas of the curriculum can be explored and children can work at their own level or in a group.

Language
Learning new songs and poems aids vocabulary. Festivals offer an introduction to new languages and an opportunity for group discussion.

Aesthetic and spiritual
Festivals are aesthetically beautiful and can be spiritually uplifting. Children have the opportunity to create objects, use new textures and explore new materials.

Sensory
A festival is a feast for the senses: the smell and taste of different foods, the light and dark of Divali, the new musical experiences, and the rich tapestry of materials.

- Celebrating festivals can dominate the curriculum if so many are chosen that little time is left for any other part of the curriculum. Plan carefully in advance, being clear about the educational purpose and the relevance of the celebration.
- Remember that some families may not wish their children to take part in festivals, either due to their own religion or to their very strong anti-religious beliefs. Before embarking on a festival celebration, check with the families first, and find out those who do not wish to participate, and those who wish to become involved. If you do have children who are not going to take part, make sure that you have an appropriate alternative activity for them, and respect their wish not to be involved.
- Consult closely with parents or leaders of religious communities, to make sure that you have the correct information. Not all members of an ethnic or religious group will celebrate in the same way, and you must ensure that you do not offend or distress anyone.
- Any clothes or artefacts lent by parents must be handled carefully, but parents must be made aware that accidents can happen.
- If you have one or two children to represent the culture or religion you are celebrating, be careful not to continually single them out as you may embarrass them.
- Hallowe'en is not a suitable festival for very young children. There is no point in frightening children with horrific tales of witches and evil doings.

Essential points

Equal opportunities

- There is a risk of stereotyping if you celebrate festivals too extravagantly, and concentrate on the exotic side of their beliefs or culture. Respecting other cultures and religions should be an every day occurrence, not a once a year wonder.

Safety

- Any festivals which celebrate light with open candles such as Divali and Hanukah need very careful supervision.
- Most Guy Fawkes celebrations are very well monitored these days, although one still hears of death and injury. In the school or nursery situation, it is unwise to have fireworks, and Guy Fawkes should only be remembered in verse, story and craft work. A discussion group could be held with teachers, parents and children, warning of the dangers of fireworks, of walking the street asking for money for the guy, and of trick-or-treating on Hallowe'en.

Resources

Addis I. and Spooner S., 1994, *Assemblies*, Scholastic Publications Ltd.

Ashraf S. A., 1995, *Islam, Teachers' Manual*, Westhill Project, Westhill R.E. Centre.

Breuillx B. and Palmer M., 1993, *Sainsbury's Religions of the World*, Harper Collins.

Carey D. and Large J., 1982, *Festivals, Families and Food*, Hawthorne Press.

Court C., 1993, *Festivals*, Scholastic Publications Ltd.

Deshpande C., 1985, *Diwali*, Celebrations Series, A. & C. Black (Publishers) Ltd.

East H. (compiler), 1989, *The Singing Sack: songs and stories from around the world*, A. & C. Black (Publishers) Ltd, (cassette also available).

Fitzjohn S., Weston M. and Large J., 1993, *Festivals Together*, Hawthorn Press.

Fitzsimmons J. and Whiteford R., 1993, *Festivals and Celebrations*, Bright Ideas for Early Years Series, Scholastic Publications Ltd.

Gilbert J., 1986, *Festivals*, OUP.

Godfrey S., 1990, *Christmas Activities*, Bright Ideas for Early Years Series, Scholastic Publications Ltd.

Hannigan L., 1985, *Sam's Passover*, A. & C. Black (Publishers) Ltd.

Misrahi B., 'Celebrating Religions in the Nursery' in *Nursery World*, 14 December 1989

Montagu S., 1990, *Judaism, Teachers' Manual*, Westhill Project, Stanley Thornes (Publishers) Ltd.

Palmer J., 1993, *Festivals*, Blueprint Series, Stanley Thornes (Publishers) Ltd.

Read G., Rudge J. and Howarth R. B., 1995, *Christianity, Teachers' Manual*, Westhill Project, Westhill R.E. Centre.

Rosen M., 1990, *Autumn, Winter, Spring*, and *Summer*, Seasonal Festivals Series, Wayland Publishers Ltd.

Sharp E., *Working Party on World Religions in Education*, National Society for Religious Education, from the Society's R.E. Centre, 36 Causton Street, London SW1P 4AU. Telephone 0171 932 1194

Store S., 1988, *Eid ul-Fitr*, A. & C. Black (Publishers) Ltd.

Bridges to Religions, 1994, Warwick R.E. Project, Heinemann.

Dolls and dressing-up clothes: see references to J. and M. Toys and Ann Johnson, page 35.

15 *Information Technology*

Because of the growing importance of computers it is probable that you will come across them in many of your placements. Information technology is listed within the learning outcomes under 'knowledge and understanding of the world'. You may have a personal computer (PC) at home, and be conversant with the multi-media skills required. It is likely that you will have access to computers at your college, and you should take full advantage of any training offered.

Some pre-schools and schools will have state of the art equipment and software, whilst others have rather antiquated machines, but in most placements the children will be offered the opportunity to use them. They will bring into the school or nursery a variety of experiences, some children being very familiar with the computer from home, whilst for others it may be their first opportunity to use the equipment. Those of you who are not confident in your use of computers will be learning alongside the children. An interested and positive approach is desirable, and if you feel anxiety you must do your best not to communicate it.

Some educationalists have suggested that using computers at a very young age may not be all that appropriate, as there are many other social and physical skills to be learnt, and computers can be isolating and time-consuming. No child should be encouraged or allowed to spend long periods of time at the computer.

As with videos and television, it is the way the computers are used and the interaction of the adult that results in a satisfactory activity that extends the children's learning.

AMOUNT OF SPACE		TYPE OF SPACE	
Whole area		Outside	
Half area		Inside	
Quarter area		Hard surface	
Small area	■	Carpeted	
		Table space	■
TYPE OF PLAY	■	**INVOLVEMENT OF ADULT**	
Solitary	■	Essential	
Parallel		Enriching	■
Small group		Not always necessary	■
Large group		Can be intrusive	

ESSENTIAL EQUIPMENT
Computer with monitor, mouse and keyboard
Built in software
Instruction manual
Table and chair of a comfortable height

SUGGESTED ADDITIONAL EQUIPMENT
Printer and paper
CD-ROMs and additional software with storage
Floppy disks, with storage
Mouse pad
Multi-media speaker system
Digital camera
Scanner
Microphone
Joystick
Modem
Lower case keyboard

Good Practice

- Make sure that no food, drink, sand or water is allowed near the computer.
- Ensure the children understand the rules of behaviour before allowing them to use the computer.
- Make the computer area look attractive, perhaps by displaying posters and information.
- Over a period of time, all children should have an opportunity to use the computer.
- Keep a record of which children have had time on the computer and what programmes they have used.
- Always use the correct computer terminology.
- The ink in the printer should be checked regularly, particularly if the children are printing out pictures in colour. Make sure there is sufficient paper in stock.
- Have patience and take time to explain the computing process.
- Ask for help if you cannot sort a problem quickly.
- Cover the computer and printer at the end of each session.

VALUE TO AREAS OF DEVELOPMENT AND LEARNING

Physical
Fine manipulative skills and hand-eye co-ordination are promoted when using the mouse or the keyboard.

Social and moral
Using the computer is usually a solitary occupation, but two children sometimes work together, although only one at a time can use the mouse. This encourages taking turns, sharing ideas and problem solving together. There are CD ROMS that look at social and ethical issues in a way that older children can understand. Support has to be frequently sought and given.

Emotional
Some games on the computer are competitive, and children have to learn how to lose gracefully and not gloat when they win. Self-esteem and confidence are gained with the successful completion of a programme. Using the computer can, and should be, an enjoyable activity. Patience and perseverance are learnt when problems occur.

Intellectual
Using a computer aids concentration and problem solving. It can be used as a tool for gaining literacy and numeracy skills. Exploration and experimentation are encouraged. Some games demand auditory discrimination, and most require visual discrimination. Older children are able to access the Internet for information and research, and test theories.

Language
Listening skills are developed, as understanding instructions is a vital part of computer expertise. Vocabulary is extended, as the language of computers has to be learnt.

Aesthetic and spiritual
Children can experiment with the paintbox, creating patterns and pictures, using sprays, brushes and pencils. There are CD ROMS for young artists that encourage creativity and colour experimentation.

Sensory
Using a computer is a tactile experience. When pictures are created, they can be visually pleasing.

Send for some software catalogues featuring CD ROMS suitable for young children.

1 What might you select to support the six areas of early learning goals (see page 4)?
2 What might be suitable to support the National Curriculum?
3 What games do you think have little to commend them? Why?

Essential points

Equal opportunities

- Some children will have frequent access to computers in the home and you may need to give priority to those children who have had little or no experience before attending the nursery or school.
- Research has shown that even in these enlightened times boys are encouraged to use computers more than girls. You need to be aware that there might be this imbalance and to redress it if necessary.
- All software should show positive images of all cultures and both genders, and needs to be scrutinised for possible bias.
- Computers operated by various parts of the body can present learning opportunities for children with physical disabilities allowing access to the wider world. Programmes, which teach in small steps, can be helpful to children with learning difficulties.

Safety

- All equipment needs to have appropriate plugs professionally fitted and there should be access to a number of power points.
- Computer cables should be stored out of the way of children.
- The monitor should be at an angle that makes children look up slightly when they are using it.
- The chairs should have backs and be high enough for the children to keep their lower arms straight.
- Wrists should be supported on the table or keyboard shelf.
- Never allow the children to play with the back of the equipment or linking cables.
- Ensure that every piece of equipment is switched off at the end of the day.

Resources

Doherty G., 1998, *101 Things to do with Your Computer*, Usborne.

Dungworth R., 1996, *Windows for Beginners*, Usborne Computer Guides.

James F. and Kerr A., 1997, *Creative Computing*, Belair Publications.

Kalbag A., 1997, *World Wide Web for Beginners*, Usborne Computer Guides.

Polly J A., 1997, *Internet – Kids and Family*, Osborne/McGraw Hill, 2nd edition.

Stephens M. and Treays R., 1994, revised 1997, *Computers for Beginners*, Usborne.

Wheeler T. and Short R., 1997, *101 Amazing Things to do with Your Computer*, Kingfisher.

Wingate P. and Kalbag A., 1998, *The Usborne Complete Book of the Internet and World Wide Web*, Usborne.

Part 3

Activities for Babies

0 to 1 Year and Toddlers 1 to 2 Years

For babies and toddlers, play is just as important as it is for older children. It is sometimes not fully realised that babies need activities and a bored baby may become an unhappy baby. Some babies may cry when they do not have enough to do, and a worthwhile activity will distract the baby, and has more value than a pacifier, such as a rocking chair or a dummy.

Part 3 looks at the need for stimulation of very young children, and how best to offer a variety of activities to babies and toddlers. We discuss the areas of development in more detail. The format is similar to Part 2, pointing out good practice and emphasising the need for safety with the youngest children.

16 *Babies 0 to 1 Year*

Babies are learning and developing as soon as they are born – many would say from the moment of conception. The neonate quickly learns to recognise the face, the smell, the feel, the taste and the voice of the mother, thus using all the senses to ensure survival.

Development

In addition to love, protection, shelter, and food the baby also needs stimulation. At first the mother provides all the stimulation the baby requires, through gentle handling and stroking, speaking in a soft voice, and feeding on demand.

As the baby develops, the interaction between the mother or main caregiver and the baby becomes increasingly important. The babies routine becomes more established, and there is time to play when feeding, bathing and changing napkins. Many babies are spending larger parts of the day awake, and this is a time to truly interact, and to ensure that the baby is not left alone and bored.

Encouraging development

By six weeks, most babies are smiling, showing that they are responding to a stimulus, usually during a conversation whilst maintaining good eye contact. This is the time to introduce other stimuli, such as mobiles and rattles. The mobiles which will interest the baby most will have the pictures positioned so that the baby can gaze at them when lying supine in the crib or cot, or lying back in a bouncing cradle. Bright colours add interest, and some have a musical attachment. They can be bought or home made. Babies also learn by taking all objects to their mouths, so rattles and other toys must be carefully checked for safety: durable, well made, non-toxic, no sharp edges, and impossible to swallow.

By far the most important stimulus is still the consistent contact given to the baby by parents, siblings, grandparents and other familiar adults. Interacting with songs and cuddles and talking to the baby will aid emotional, cognitive and language development. The first response will be facial – smiles and intense looks. Be sure to take turns, and listen to the baby when he or she begins to vocalise.

After changing the baby's napkin, allow some time for play with hands and feet, unrestricted by clothing. Most babies enjoy their bathtimes, getting pleasure from the warmth of the water and the freedom to kick and splash. This aids all-round development.

Describe in detail the areas of development that are extended by bathtime.

At around six weeks, babies can be seen occasionally moving their hands towards objects in their field of vision, and sometimes accidentally succeeding in touching them. At three months, the baby discovers his or her hands and begins to engage in finger play. By six months, this area of hand-eye coordination is usually well established and babies can reach out for an object they desire, and grasp it. Initially, toys such as activity centres which hang suspended just within the baby's reach, will help develop this skill. Playmats with a range of different sensory activities will help stimulate the baby's interest.

Increasingly, baby's responses are no longer just reflex reactions to sensory stimuli, but become selective, choosing which stimulus to react to. Lightweight rattles and toys which can be easily held in the hand, help further to develop hand-eye coordination.

When the baby is able to sit up with support, other toys can be offered. The baby will enjoy knocking down towers built of plastic or foam bricks, banging saucepan lids with a wooden spoon and having fun with weighted or suction toys that stay within the babies reach.

Singing to a baby comes naturally to most parents and caregivers. From action songs to finger rhymes, from nursery rhymes to lullabies, baby will get pleasure from them all, and enjoy a sense of security and comfort. Singing helps babies to discriminate sounds, and anticipate repetitive actions.

Reading to a small baby sometimes seems rather incongruous, but the baby will enjoy the close contact, and start to recognise familiar objects seen in picture books. It is a useful introduction to the world of books and exposure to 'book' language.

Some very simple games are enjoyable to play with very young babies. Lying the baby on a playmat or bean bag, you might:

■ make eye contact with the baby. Take the baby's hands and let the baby feel your face whilst you talk and sing
■ hold an object in front of the baby, and move it from side to side encouraging the baby to follow it. From about six weeks encourage the baby to reach out for the object, remembering to talk and praise the baby
■ move the baby's legs in a cycling movement
■ clap the baby's hands together
■ massage and stroke the baby

Other activities to stimulate the baby include
■ playing 'Peek-a-boo'
■ placing the baby prone, placing toys in front of him or her to encourage head control at first, and movement at a later stage.

Emotional development

Some babies are very demanding of attention, and cry each time they are left on their own, whilst others settle quite happily by themselves, perhaps playing with their hands or feet. All babies should be picked up when they cry and never left to 'cry it out'. Less demanding babies also need attention and stimulating play-activities should be offered. Babies need to make close emotional attachments and, if in day care, should be cared for by as few people as possible, ideally by a 'key worker'. The parents will tell you which songs, activities and rhymes the baby enjoys.

Intellectual development

Babies develop intelligence mainly through their senses. Once babies are mobile, curiosity about their environment is paramount, and they should be allowed to explore as much as they wish, always ensuring they are safe and not exposed to hazards. Continually talking and listening to babies' vocalisations helps encourage early language development, and the first words may start to appear at the end of the first year.

Becoming mobile

During the first year of life, the baby will have developed physical control, sitting first with and then without support, rolling, creeping and crawling, pulling to stand and taking the first few hand-held steps. Some may be walking confidently by their first birthday, whilst others may need encouragement to get started, and there are many toys you can provide, such as baby walkers, trucks and trolleys which can be pushed along. Walkers, in which you sit the baby, are unsafe and have been known to cause many accidents.

Encouraging sensory development: the treasure basket

All areas of sensory development can be encouraged by the use of a treasure basket, as described by Elinor Goldschmied. The baby is offered a container filled with objects made of natural materials, none of them plastic or recognisable as 'toys'.

AMOUNT OF SPACE		TYPE OF SPACE	
Whole area		Outside	■
Half area		Inside	■
Quarter area		Hard surface	
Small area	■	Carpeted	■
		Table space	
TYPE OF PLAY		**INVOLVEMENT OF ADULT**	
Solitary	■	Essential	
Parallel		Enriching	
Small group		Not always necessary	
Large group		Can be intrusive	■

ESSENTIAL MATERIALS FOR THE TREASURE BASKET

Container, preferably a basket, large enough to hold at least 20 items
Cushion or bean bag, so as to support the baby comfortably on the floor
Rug, if used outside
About 20 items to stimulate the five senses, such as a plastic baby-mirror, an orange, a fir cone, a piece of pumice, a small natural sponge, tissue paper, a large stone, small cloth bags containing lavender or cloves, a brush, a piece of velvet, clothes pegs, and a bunch of keys

SUGGESTED ADDITIONAL EQUIPMENT

Any natural object, as long as it is safe for the baby to play with.
There is an excellent chapter in *People Under Three* by Elinor Goldschmied and Sonia Jackson, giving many further suggestions.

Activity

Plan a treasure basket. List five items for each of the senses.

Good Practice

- All the equipment must be kept clean, and perishable objects such as fruit, need to be discarded and replaced as necessary.
- The baby should be allowed to explore the items without any adult intervention or encouragement. Adults should supervise from a distance and not talk or interact with the baby, as this will interfere with the baby's concentration.
- Items should be changed or washed fairly often so as to continually stimulate exploratory play.
- A comfortable and safe position for the baby must be found, so that the baby does not topple over and become distracted.
- If the baby is using the basket among a group of older, mobile children, care must be taken to ensure that the older children do not spoil the activity by handling or taking away the objects. A heavy stone, for example, whilst pleasant for the baby to touch, might turn into a lethal weapon in the hands of an older child.

VALUE TO AREAS OF DEVELOPMENT AND LEARNING

Physical
The treasure basket develops large muscles in the arms when stretching for items in the basket, and in waving and shaking them. It provides practice in sitting without being held, and develops hand-eye coordination when manipulating small objects.

Social and moral
This is usually a solitary activity, but if more than one baby is using the basket, there may be some interplay.

Emotional
Exploring the treasure basket is a satisfying experience. Tension may be released through banging objects. An activity carried out by the baby alone, leading to independent playing.

Intellectual
It aids concentration and exploratory play. The baby begins to understand the different qualities of various items of equipment and starts to make choices and decisions.

Aesthetic and spiritual
This leads to an appreciation of attractive natural objects.

Sensory
It is essentially an activity designed to extend to all the senses.

Essential points

Equal opportunities

The treasure basket
- Babies could be introduced to exotic smells, objects and materials from all round the world.
- This is a gender-free activity.
- Older children with special needs who are unable to move around freely, will gain stimulation from a treasure basket.

- Care must be taken when selecting the items for the treasure basket, checking to see that there are no sharp edges, nothing is too heavy, and nothing small enough to swallow or insert into noses and ears.
- All toys and equipment given to a baby should be clean and need to be washable to avoid infection. They should be durable to avoid accidents from broken edges, and any painted items should be covered in non-toxic paint. They should conform to safety standards.
- Small babies are vulnerable to suffocation, so avoid using pillows and cushions, and ensure that any plastic bags are stored out of the baby's reach.
- Anything with strings should not be near the baby as, if the string becomes wrapped around the neck or other parts of the body, the blood supply could be cut off, or the child could be hanged.
- Be careful with heavy toys or objects near the baby.
- Always supervise floor play.
- Make sure the baby's environment is safe and hazard free.

Resources

Dare A. and O'Donovan M., 1998, *A Practical Guide to Working with Babies*, 2nd edition, Stanley Thornes (Publishers) Ltd.

Emerson S., 1992, *Baby Games and Lullabies*, Kingfisher Books.

Goldschmied E. and Jackson S., 1994, *People Under Three*, Routledge.

Goldschmied E. and Selleck D., 1996, *Communication Between Babies in their First Year*, NCB (a video is included with this training book).

Leach P., 1983, *Babyhood*, Penguin Books.

Miller L., 1992, *Understanding Your Baby*, Rosendale Press.

Petrie P., 1987, *Baby Play*, Century Hutchinson.

Sheridan M., 1977, *Spontaneous Play in Early Childhood*, NFER.

17 Toddlers 1 to 2 Years

When working with this age group, you will find it useful to look at each area of development, and the activities and toys which will help promote and extend this development.

Development

Toddlers are challenging, and often the toys and activities provided by the adults may be used in a very different way by the child from that expected by the adult, but this is acceptable as learning is still taking place, and toddlers should be given every opportunity to explore and set their own agenda within a safe environment.

Physical development

Encouraging physical skills (large body movements)

Balls of all sizes, made out of various materials, stimulate a toddler to move, and extend the mobility of children who are already walking, aiding their balance and coordination. As the toddler becomes more proficient at walking, pull-along toys are fun, and encourage children to walk for a longer period. Once children are mobile, and walking confidently, the next stage is learning and practising skills and exploring the environment.

Suggestions for children between 1 and 2 years include a staircase on which toddlers should be shown initially how to climb upstairs, and more importantly, how to crawl down; and a small slide to practise climbing skills. Sliding down is the reward!

'Hidey hole' boxes or large wooden cubes, which are sturdy and large enough for toddlers to climb in, promote skills of getting in and out of objects, coordination and balance. Strong supermarket cartons are an acceptable alternative.

Wheeled toys to sit on, and move with the feet, encourage the practice of steering skills, balance, and coordination and help to strengthen leg muscles.

A low climbing frame aids balance and coordination and strengthens arm and leg muscles as do balls, for throwing, catching and kicking.

Outings to parks, where the playground will have swings, seesaws, roundabouts and rocking toys, are enjoyable. Here, children can use the equipment according to their own individual skills, under close supervision.

Encouraging fine manipulative skills

During the first year, babies start to practise the skills of handling and manipulating small objects, reaching and grasping, holding and letting go, moving objects from hand to hand, passing objects, poking and pointing with one finger, and picking up objects with finger and thumb. There are many materials that will help develop manipulative skills and hand-eye coordination such as bricks for building towers that can be knocked down; stacking cups and beakers; small tins and cartons that can be improvised from around the house; posting boxes; hammer sets; dolls that are easily undressed; and simple inset jigsaws.

The contents of the lower kitchen cupboards, where it is sensible to store only safe sturdy equipment, such as saucepans, plastic storage containers, baking tins and wooden spoons, can be played with as well as small bouncy balls, Duplo, large threading toys such as cotton reels and large wooden beads, and screw toys. Playdough, crayons, and finger paints can be used.

Activity

Obtain catalogues from at least four different manufacturers, and select what seems to you to be the best outdoor equipment for a toddler, so as to promote all-round physical development.

Social and moral development

Up to the age of 1 year, apart from interaction with the prime caregiver, there is little social development, and no sign of any moral development, but as a foundation for moral development, the consistency and firmness of the caregivers in handling the behaviour of the toddler will ensure a good start.

During the second year, as the child becomes mobile and understands more, he or she has to learn how to fit happily into the family and the larger outside environment and a whole set of rules has to be learnt about acceptable behaviour. At this stage, play is solitary, but the presence of a familiar adult provides reassurance and security. A toddler is not interested in playing cooperatively with other children. He or she has just learnt the meaning of 'mine', and the concept of sharing usually does not occur until the third year.

Encouraging social development

Introducing toddlers to the wider environment will help them come to terms with the outside world. As well as outings to visit the family, walks in the park, perhaps meeting other small children to play alongside, and leisurely expeditions to local shops where a conversation might take place, will all help the toddler understand his or her role in the community.

Parent and toddler groups, toy libraries, visits to the local library, drop-in centres, and clinics where other small children are likely to be found, will enlarge the social circle.

Provision of small scale household equipment, such as brooms and vacuum cleaners, allows the toddler to imitate the main caregiver, and encourages the beginning of role play.

Emotional development

During the first year, the baby has progressed emotionally from total dependency to an understanding that there are some things he or she is able to do on his or her own, and this increases during the second year. You will need to have patience as the toddler tries to help you with their own care or the chores.

It is often possible to avoid confrontations, but if these do take place, toddlers are usually quite amenable to diversions. Some feelings are so strong and overpowering that you just have to wait until the storm has passed and then cuddle and comfort the child, who may well be frightened by the immensity of these emotions. A great deal depends on the developing personality of the child, as to how happy or sad he or she may be. Comfort objects, such as dummies, blankets, a special soft toy, or any other item to which the child is particularly attached, play a large part in their lives, and no attempt should be made to remove them.

It is best to have as few rules as possible, and to make sure that the environment is safe and offers security.

Although toddlers are stepping out into the wider world, they still need the love and support of a familiar adult, and find new emotional demands difficult to deal with. You need to be aware of this when first building a relationship with a child of this age, and proceed slowly and sensitively.

Encouraging emotional development

Messy play, such as finger painting or play with wet clay, dough, water, wet sand, mud, cornflour or cooked pasta will soothe upset children and allow an outlet for aggressive feelings.

Outings and vigorous play outside help children to release pent-up feelings and tire them out, so that they will sleep better at night.

Bathtimes help children to unwind at the end of the day.

If you give time for toddlers to feed themselves and let them help to dress and undress themselves, you will find that they soon become quite skilled.

Toddlers can start to make decisions, but it is best just to give them two choices, such as 'Would you like ravioli or fish fingers for dinner?'

Intellectual and language development

Children learn at an amazing rate, and during the first year, the baby has learnt, among other things, to become mobile, to understand a great deal of what is said, to speak a few words, to identify people they are in regular contact with, and to recognise food they enjoy. The next year shows an acceleration of learning as the toddler becomes more proficient with language.

Although play is mainly solitary, the toddler spends an increasingly large proportion of time in exploratory and experimental play, in looking at books, listening to, and taking part in songs and rhymes, learning that objects have names, as do parts of the body, and realising that by using language, needs are met without having recourse to pointing and whingeing.

Encouraging intellectual and language development

The child should have access to a good selection of picture books, many of which can be handled alone, and a repertoire of finger plays, songs, action rhymes, nursery rhymes, and verse.

Opportunities should be found for conversation and good communication, taking time to listen as well as talk. Providing interest tables, displaying pictures and posters, and allowing toddlers to handle objects; all these things will stimulate their curiousity, as well as helping to extend their vocabulary. You will need to gain a sound theoretical understanding of language acquisition to ensure you promote this important area of development.

There are many toys on the market for children of this age. The most essential are bricks and blocks. (Duplo, foam blocks and plastic bricks do less harm than wooden ones if thrown around.) Posting boxes and similar toys encourage hand-eye co-ordination, memory and concentration.

Children gain a great deal of pleasure and learning from bath toys, where early concepts of floating, sinking, volume and capacity may be learnt.

Small scale domestic equipment, such as telephones, brooms and tea sets can be provided to encourage imitative play.

Heuristic play

This type of play was devised by Elinor Goldschmied for groups of toddlers and is particularly suitable for children in daycare. It is intended as an enrichment of the children's play, and the staff have to be committed to carrying it out on a regular basis.

Fifteen bags need to be provided, and each bag should have enough of the same objects for all the children in the group. The contents might include bulldog clips, corks, springs, curlers, short pieces of chain, old keys, cardboard tubes, extra large curtain rings, tins and lids, small boxes, and anything else that a toddler would safely enjoy exploring. Receptacles should be provided for the children.

The role of the adult is to provide the objects and keep them clean and in good order. They should not participate in the play in any way, but just sit quietly at the side of the room, which has been emptied of all furniture and equipment. The children enter this empty space, and start exploring the objects in the bags. The activity can go on for forty minutes, thoroughly engrossing the children in the same way that the treasure basket did for less mobile children. Toddlers have an increasing desire to explore and experiment, and heuristic play satisfies this need. Workers in daycare centres are enthusiastic about heuristic play, as it is seen to be satisfying and enjoyable for the toddlers, and allows the adults to observe the development of the children.

Aesthetic and spiritual development

This may be the age when the foundation is laid for later creativity and appreciation of the world around us. Maria Montessori felt very deeply about this, and always had beautiful pictures on the walls and glorious materials draped around the room. She felt that the children's work was not aesthetically beautiful enough to be displayed.

Encouraging aesthetic and spiritual development

Provide some well-crafted wooden toys. Encourage painting and drawing, which from an early age allows children to express their creativity. Have beautifully illustrated books. Provide an introduction to music and outings that will introduce the child to the wonders of the natural world. Blow bubbles!

Sensory development

Very young children learn mainly through their senses. As they grow older, learning in this way becomes less dominant. Toddlers, not yet in full command of language, use all their senses spontaneously in exploratory and experimental play. It is important that this is allowed and not discouraged by caregivers, telling them not to put objects in their mouths, or not to touch something which may not be completely hygienic, such as mud. In general, toddlers will explore everything through the senses, as this is instinctive, but there is a need to encourage children who may have some sensory impairment.

Essential points

Equal opportunities

- With the toddler's increasing understanding of language, it is important that you choose books which show positive images of all cultures, of both sexes, and show disabled people in leading roles.
- At this age, children start to realise what gender they are, and this is important to them. Toddlers should be encouraged to play with all toys and try out every type of activity, and not just provided with toys and activities thought to be suitable for one gender only.

Safety

- Toddlers always need to be closely supervised. Their natural curiosity and adventurousness will lead them into potentially dangerous activities, so their environment needs to be as hazard-free as possible. All toys and equipment need to be durable and bought from a reputable manufacturer, and need to be checked for damage, maintained and repaired if necessary. Make sure that anything they are playing with cannot be swallowed or inserted into ears or up noses.
- With the beginning of language, toddlers will understand when you say no, and you can start to teach them the rules of safety, but remember that understanding these rules will relate to the age and stage of development of the child.
- Remember to:
  - provide safety gates on stairs and at the entrance to the kitchen
  - provide fixed fire and cooker guards
  - provide plug guards
  - ensure harmful substances, such as bleach and medication, are locked up out of reach
  - ensure gates and doors to the outside are locked

- ensure the child cannot lock him or herself in the freezer, fridge, bathroom, garden shed, or any area where there may be danger
- use a harness in pram, high-chair and pushchair
- use reins in the street
- never leave a baby or toddler alone in the bath or the car or outside a shop
- never leave hot drinks within reach of a baby or a toddler.

Resources

Butler D., 1988, *Babies Need Books*, Penguin Books.

Cass-Beggs B., 1978, *Your Baby Needs Music*, Ward Lockhead.

Corbett P. and Emerson S., 1992, *Dancing and Singing Games*, Kingfisher Books.

Gee R. and Meredith S., 1989, *Entertaining and Educating Babies and Toddlers*, Parents' Guide Series, Usborne Publishing.

Goldschmied E. and Hughes A., 1992, *Heuristic Play with Objects*, NCB.

Goldschmied E. and Jackson S., 1994, *People Under Three*, Routledge.

Petrie P., 1989, *Communicating with Children and Adults*, Edward Arnold.

Thompson J., 1997, *Toddler Care Day by Day*, Harper Collins.

Part 4

Course Work

The satisfactory completion of practical work with children is required by various childcare courses of all levels, many having different regulations and requirements. This applies to college-based courses and National Vocational Qualifications. In Part 4, we have attempted to outline some of the different regulations. We have also tried to clarify some of the practical course work required, so that you will understand in advance what is expected of you.

We have included guidance on how to evaluate your work, as this is an intrinsic part of becoming a professional childcare practitioner.

18 *Course Work*

Most childcare courses require you to plan, prepare, implement and evaluate activities for the children in your placement. You may be on a course where you will have to plan your activities in detail. For example, the CACHE course leading to a Diploma in Child Care and Education (DCE) requires you to submit a number of curriculum plans, detailed activity plans, and routines, put together in a portfolio. This is a longitudinal unit of the DCE, known as Unit 2.

For the CACHE Certificate in Childcare and Education course (CCE) you will be asked to undertake a number of planned activities that will be included in your portfolio.

As CACHE requirements may change from year to year, we have not attempted to outline all the regulations. These will be found in your overview, and your tutors will give you the necessary information, help and support in understanding the structure of the course.

By reading this chapter, we hope that you can begin to understand what will be required of you in placement and have included some examples for you to consider.

Curriculum plans

'Curriculum' is the term used to describe all the learning that takes place in any setting. A curriculum plan describes the range of activities or experiences offered to children to promote specific areas of learning and development, leading to appropriate outcomes according to the age of the child. See pages 124–128 for an example of a curriculum plan written by a DCE student in her second term.

The reason students are asked to write curriculum plans is so that they can plan activities confidently, recognising where and how learning occurs whilst incorporating equality of opportunity and responding to the total development and learning needs of the child. They learn how to plan, carry out and evaluate activities and how to keep records that can be shared with the team and the parents. As students recognise and understand their own contribution to the learning process, they become more secure in their professional role.

When you devise a curriculum plan you will need to be clear about the aim and rationale of the plan, and the anticipated learning outcomes for both the child and yourself. You will be expected to describe briefly a number of activities related to the plan, each outlining a different learning objective within the plan.

CURRICULUM PLAN – Imaginative play

Date: 8/2/99

Length of plan: Two weeks

Briefly describe the experience/activity/routine:
A series of activities/experiences designed to
promote and extend children's all-round development
through imaginary play.

Venue: A nursery class in a primary school.

No. of children: 25

Age/s of children: 3-4:11 years

Gender: Male and female

Culture: Mixture of English, Spanish,
African-Caribbean and Turkish

**Planning and organisation (including resources, space and adults
involved):** Age-appropriate resources and experiences,
indoor and outdoor space, one adult involved.

Concepts/language to be introduced: Health and safety
environment, extension of vocabulary, metamorphosis
of food, temperature, time.

Details of parents/carers, staff present: One nursery teacher,
one child-care and education worker, one student.

Time started: 8/2/99

Time finished: 22/2/99

Example of a curriculum plan front page

CURRICULUM PLAN DETAILS

Area of the room	Experience/Activity	Skills/Knowledge	Early years learning outcomes	Adult role	Resources
Graphics	Collage using a wide variety of materials Drawing with a variety of felt tips	Develops hand–eye co-ordination Gives visual and tactile experience Stimulates imagination and aesthetic awareness Encourages exploration and experimentation Develops pencil control Valuable means of expression	Physical Language/literacy Aesthetic/creative Personal/social	Structure materials to encourage incidental learning and self-expression Observe the use of space, time and materials	Coloured paper, sequins, felt, PVA glue, scissors, coloured pasta and rice A4 paper and felt tips (both fat and thin)
Creative	Modelling with clay Modelling with recyclable materials	Develops manipulative skills Develops gross and fine motor skills Develops individual inventiveness Encourages sharing materials and taking turns Encourages creativity, a sense of achievement and self-esteem	Physical Personal/social Aesthetic/creative Maths Language/literacy	Careful presentation and protection can help to avoid unnecessary mess and potential hazards Support children's intentions Provide options and choices Extend the range of materials and resources	Clay, shape cutters, rolling pins, protective clothing Space for drying Variety of boxes, containers, dispensers and cardboard tubes PVA glue, scissors Ready mixed paint – various colours
Construction	Large wooden building block Medium size tool set Miniature train set	Develops both gross and fine motor skills Develops hand–eye co-ordination Provides a stimulus for both group and individual play Develops fine co-ordination as well as careful observation skills	Physical Personal/social Maths Language/literacy	Provide a balance between too little detail and too much Encourage conversation between children Facilitate on-going play	Realistic and size-related sets Large wooden blocks Space in carpeted area Trains, tracks, small world toys Tool set
Mathematics	Cooking – making vegetable soup Turn the Home Corner into a surgery	Learning about measuring, numbers and how they fit into everyday life Encourages exploration of different textures and smells Provides experience of how changes occur in materials Encourages a grasp of concepts of numbers, counting and sorting Develops hand–eye co-ordination and discrimination Develops language. Turn-taking is encouraged	Maths Physical Knowledge/understanding Personal/social Language/literacy	Allow opportunities to experience adult roles giving adequate guidance and observing health and safety rules Provide for every stage of interest and ability Use subtle observation techniques	Table, utensils, ingredients, cooker Table, bed, chairs, doctor's instruments, nurses uniform, bandages, cotton wool, posters, syringes, appointment diaries
Science	Graded containers in the water tray Wet sand tray with buckets and trowels Dry sand tray with dinosaurs	Develops learning about volume – larger/smaller than Develops hand–eye co-ordination and visual perception Develops language and communication skills Gives tactile experiences	Maths Physical Knowledge/understanding Language/literacy	Introduce idea of judging quantity Provide aprons to protect clothes Discuss differences in textures: wet/dry, smooth/rough	Graded plastic jugs and funnels also tubing of similar capacity but different shapes Buckets and trowels Plastic dinosaurs
Outdoor	Collect frogspawn to hatch into tadpoles Bulb planting	Develops a sense of time and gives valuable experiences of caring and looking after something smaller than themselves Encourages questions about how things grow Develops language skills and thought	Maths Aesthetic/creative Physical Knowledge/understanding Language/literacy	Visit a pond to see frogs in their natural environment Walk around the local park to see flowers and develop the concepts of time and change	Pond, small fishing nets, fish tank Flower pots, soil, variety of bulbs, name labels, trowels Space
Carpet	Story session 'On the Way Home' with the use of story props	Develops manipulative control when turning pages Encourages turn-taking when asking questions Aids imagination Encourages concentration Extends knowledge of the world Develops new vocabulary and fosters listening skills	Physical Personal/social Language/literacy Aesthetic/creative Knowledge/understanding	Allow time for discussion afterwards Promote a positive world view – make sure books are not racist/sexist or have stereo-typical assumptions about gender roles and those with special needs Encourage heritage languages	Chair for adult Carpeted area Magnetic board and story props Book

<u>**CURRICULUM PLAN**</u>

INTRODUCTION

Based around the theme of imaginative play, approximately fourteen appropriate activities and experiences, will be implemented during 2 weeks. These are intended to promote children's learning and development through: language activities - speaking and listening; mathematical activities - counting, sorting, number operation; knowledge and understanding of the world - scientific aspect of cooking and the changes which occur; personal and social experiences - role play, turn-taking games; and creative activities - developing fine and gross motor skills, and hand-eye co-ordination.

This curriculum plan is designed for 24 children aged 3 to 4:11 years in a nursery setting attached to a primary school. All the activities can be carried out by all the children in the nursery, taking into account the constraints of the setting, safety and needs of the children, parents/carers and other staff.

I will provide or suggest suitable resources for the effective implementation of activities, and utilise the available resources in the setting and the local community. The activities will enable the children to gain relevant meaningful experiences, whilst increasing their skills and competencies.

RATIONALE

Good planning in early years settings is essential so as to provide a broad, balanced and differentiated curriculum; to support the children's needs and their learning in an effective manner; and to ensure that all activities, experiences and equipment are appropriate to the children's level of development and ability.

Establishing a daily or weekly routine offers opportunities for the nursery nurse to observe, analyse and make improvements when necessary. Good planning also serves as a form of record keeping; and can be used to show parents/carers how their child's physical, intellectual, language, emotional, social, moral and spiritual needs are being met and further developed through the curriculum.

The value of play is at times underrated, but in an early years' setting it is an important part of the day; and imaginative play in particular helps to provide valuable insight into further understanding the needs of individual children. Bruce (1996) supports this view and states that, 'play is also an important contributor to the all-round development of children' and that 'children who play are more likely to be children who are resilient and continue to be resilient during adult life'. Therefore, early years practitioners will do well if we can develop the child's powers of imagination as imaginary play 'provides children with a necessary vehicle for developing wide ranging social skills, physical co-ordination and mental discipline' (*Nursery World*, 8/8/96).

I appreciate the importance of equal opportunities for all children, and have included material which not only promotes equality of opportunity for all the children but also extends understanding and promotes a positive world view. Children need to feel confident about themselves, and to be sure that they are valued. Maintaining a professional attitude at all times and commitment to equal opportunities will prevent children developing negative feelings about themselves, which could lead to a lack of self-esteem and inhibit their development. Attitudes are learnt very young, in the home, from the media and from school influences, and this is all the more reason why I should challenge stereotypes and encourage the children to experience equal opportunities in their play. All children are entitled to a clean, safe, pleasant, caring environment. I can contribute to this by being alert to hazards and giving thought to my practice. Maintaining a healthy and safe environment for the children and other members of staff requires me to know fire procedures and what to do should a fire occur, i.e. how the children are taken from the building, where our assembly point is, and where the registers are kept. I should also remain informed and up to date, in case of accidents, as to the location of the accident book, and what procedures to follow, i.e. who is responsible for notifying the parent/carer, the location of the first aid box and what it contains.

The World Health Organisation states that 'health is a state of complete physical, mental and social well-being, not merely the absence of disease or infirmity'. Therefore I should present myself as a good role model and encourage the children to see their health in a positive way i.e. to wash their hands after toileting, and before and after eating. I should also change the soiled clothing and wash any child who is wet, immediately, in order to maintain personal hygiene; and also ensure that soiled clothing is disposed of hygienically. Close supervision of potentially dangerous activities such as woodwork or cooking should be maintained at all times.

PROPOSED LEARNING OUTCOME FOR THE CHILDREN

The first activity I will implement is modelling with clay, which will take place inside the classroom on a hard surface and will require only a small space. It encourages solitary, parallel or group play. This type of modelling strengthens arm and finger muscles, and promotes fine manipulative skills. Playing in small groups encourages children to share equipment and ideas. Children may explore how clay is used by different cultures, for example in cooking and lighting equipment. Using clay encourages a range of vocabulary, e.g. 'malleable' and 'mould', and children in groups will also discuss what they are making. Clay is a tactile experience through which children can express their feelings, particularly anger and frustration, and when wet, clay can be relaxing and therapeutic to model. Natural materials like clay inspire creativity, and respect and appreciation for other children's creations should be encouraged. I will learn to keep clay in good condition so it doesn't become dry and unusuable. All tools should be in good condition and easily accessible. I intend not to interfere with the children's creativity by making models for them to copy, and not to expect an end product but just to enjoy the children's experiences, as 'natural and malleable materials are enjoyed by all age groups and are culture and gender-free experiences' (Hobart & Frankel, 1996).

Cooking, i.e. making vegetable soup, will involve the use of the kitchen next door to the classroom. This activity will develop the children's fine and gross manipulative skills when cutting up vegetables; and can lead to strong hand-eye co-ordination. The children will also learn to share equipment and utensils, take turns, develop awareness of different eating patterns and cultural diversity as well as learning safety rules. Concentration is developed by listening and following instructions. Elements of maths learning are developed through experiencing weighing, measuring, recognition of number, volume, fractions and temperature. Recipes and labelling can help children develop reading and writing skills, gain new vocabulary, learn correct terms, ask adults questions and express their needs. Science is also incorporated as children learn to appreciate the changes which take place whilst cooking. I will learn how best to involve the children in every aspect of the experience and how to be organised so that every child receives an opportunity to cook over a period of time. I intend to attempt some savoury dishes as well as sweet food to help to develop the children's tastebuds. I will also learn to plan carefully and make adequate preparations in order to ensure that I provide age-appropriate experiences. I will learn not to make stereotypical assumptions about gender or race; and to always check that all children can participate in the activity and are not prevented by diet, cultural or religious reasons. I will encourage the children to wash up and clear away afterwards; and also to relate what they have achieved to the rest of the class. I will learn to make enough food so that the whole class can enjoy the end product. This activity is ideal for dispelling any stereotypical assumptions about gender preferences as 'cooking is an experience enjoyed equally by boys and girls and presents an opportunity for them to work together' (Hobart & Frankel, 1995).

I will encourage imaginary play in the home corner by re-arranging it to look like a doctor's surgery. This will involve utilising some of the resources already there, i.e. beds, table and chairs. It will also require some additional equipment which the children should be familar with, such as stethoscopes, syringes (disposable), bandages, plasters, cotton wool, nurse's uniform, doctor's bag, small torches and wooden spatulas. I will also collect some health posters from my local clinic to put up on display for the children's information and to make the surgery more realistic. The children's gross motor skills will be developed when dressing up. Fine manipulative skills and hand-eye co-ordination is improved when used to fasten clothes, dress dolls and handle equipment. The children will experience the roles of others and social interaction is involved in playing with others. They will also develop their learning to take turns and share equipment and their caring and social skills, e.g. nursing and parenting. Imaginary play encourages exploration of different cultural backgrounds in the use of multi-cultural domestic equipment and clothes. It encourages children to express and release their emotions, both positive and negative, and to gain confidence and develop their self-esteem. Role play provides a link with home which is conforting for a child feeling insecure, or experiencing new situations. By also encouraging maths - matching and sorting - we can help children to understand concepts such as small, medium, large.

Learning to organise and direct their play, which in turn promotes creativity, stimulates children's language and communication skills and can promote discussion about life experiences. Role play is also a tactile experience when touching clothing and materials. As an early years practitioner I will learn how best to provide time, space and opportunity for this type of play, and observe discreetly, which will ensure that I facilitate and extend opportunities for role play. I will also encourage boys to use the Home Corner, and to dress up however they like. I will wait to be invited to join in and then behave as an equal to the children. I will treat clothes from other cultures with respect. The role of the adult is a sensitive one in imaginative play as 'it can be a useful window on what a child is thinking and feeling, often revealing thoughts and reactions he may not be able to put into words or would not, even if he had the vocabulary to do so' (Matterson, 1977).

I will carry out a story session on the carpet area of the classroom and include the use of story props to enhance the activity for the children. Children can develop manipulative control through turning pages, and sitting still long enough to listen encourages physical control. Reading in groups is a sharing experience and children learn to take turns when asking questions about the story and discussing the book. Empathising with a character in a book allows children to understand his or her own feelings. Books and stories allow children to use their imagination. Being able to read and understand gives a child self-esteem and a sense of achievement. Re-telling stories helps to develop memory and the ability to articulate ideas. Learning songs and rhymes also aids recall and memory; while repetitive stories and rhymes can help children with limited language skills. Attractive illustrations also help children to be aware of the beauty of the world and stimulate their imagination. It is important to always be available to read books to the children and to be aware of the needs of all the children in my group in order to promote self-esteem and feelings of self-worth. Timing is important when reading to groups of children, for example just before lunch when they're hungry or prior to going home when they feel tired or sleepy are not the best times for implementing this activity. I will allow some time for discussion afterwards.

PROPOSED LEARNING OUTCOMES FOR THE CANDIDATE

Overall, by drawing up and implementing this curriculum plan I will develop my learning of the following:
- how to encourage imaginative play
- how to plan age-appropriate activities and resources
- the importance of planning (effective time management)
- how to draw up an effective curriculum plan
- how to incorporate equal opportunities and health and safety requirements in every activity/experience
- how to utilise resources effectively in all areas of the nursery
- how activities/experiences can aid children's all-round development
- when to be involved and when to just observe
- how to choose appropriate resources for each activity
- organisational skills
- how to work in a team
- how to liase with other members of staff
- professional skills.

When drawing up a new curriculum plan, my plans will include some activities to encourage new learning experiences for both myself and the children and for a longer period – possibly a month, or a whole term. I will include music, songs and drama, as I feel these would encourage imaginative play rather than some activities (such as cooking) that I have included. I will also organise some local outings for the children which will link to the theme of the plan. Cultural issues need to be featured more prominently in the next plan. I will discuss with the children their cultural backgrounds, and whether heritage languages are spoken, before planning experiences which will reflect and celebrate the diversity in my setting.

BIBLIOGRAPHY

Bruce T., 1996, *Helping Children Learn Through Play*, Hodder & Stoughton.
Hobart C. and Frankel J., 1996, *A Practical Guide to Working with Young Children* Stanley Thornes (Publishers) Ltd.
Hobart C. and Frankel J., 1995, *A Practical Guide to Activities for Young Children*, Stanley Thornes (Publishers) Ltd.
Matterson E.M., 1977, *Play with a Purpose for Under-Sevens*, Penguin Books.

Detailed activity plans

From each curriculum plan, you will be expected to describe in detail two detailed activity plans, where you have carried out the activities with the children. See pages 130–132 for an example of a detailed activity plan.

When you have completed your activity, you should ask yourself the following questions.

1 Did you succeed in implementing your plan?
2 Did it differ in any way, and if so why?
3 How did the children react?
4 Were there any health or safety issues?
5 Did all the children have equal access?
6 Were the resources adequate?
7 Was the activity stimulating enough?
8 Was the activity too complicated?
9 Did you have enough time to carry out the activity in an unhurried fashion?
10 Did you have sufficient space?
11 Did you adequately protect the area you used?
12 Did the children learn what you thought they would learn?
13 Did they learn anything in addition?
14 Did you learn what you thought you would learn?
15 Did you learn anything else?
16 If you repeated this activity, is there anything you might do differently?
17 Did you manage to involve the children in the planning?
18 Did they willingly help you clear up after the activity?

Resources

You will be asked to produce resources that you have made yourself for some of the detailed activity plans. These might include:

- toys
- games
- musical instruments
- books
- audio tapes
- story props
- sensory materials
- mathematical or science packs
- displays or interest tables.

Your tutors will assess your resources for age-appropriateness, relevance to the activity and learning outcomes, anti-discriminatory practice, safety, durability, and presentation.

DETAILED ACTIVITY PLAN – Reading 'On the Way Home'

Date: 9/2/99

Length of plan: one day

Briefly describe the experience/activity/routine:
I am going to carry out a story session on the carpet area just after lunch. I am going to read 'On the Way Home' to a group of children and will use story props to enhance the story and make it accessible to all the children.

Venue: A nursery class in a primary school.

No. of children: Twelve

Age/s of children: 3–4:11 years

Gender: Male and female

Culture: Mixture of English, Spanish, African-Caribbean and Turkish

Planing and organisation (including resources, space and adults involved):
Large space, chair for adult, storybook, magnetic board and story props.

Concepts/language to be introduced:
Extend vocabulary, increase imagination and extend awareness of different animals.

Details of parents/carers, staff present: Two parents/carers, one nursery teacher, one student.

Time started: 12.15 pm

Time finished: 12.35 pm

Example of a detailed activity plan front page

DETAILED ACTIVITY PLAN - STORYTELLING

INTRODUCTION

This detailed plan is linked to my curriculum plan which is based around the theme of imaginary play. I will read a book called 'On the Way Home' to a group of approximately 12 children, aged 3 to 4:11 years. The book is linked to the current curriculum plan in my nursery placement and ties in with the theme of imagination. This story session will take place on the carpet area immediately after lunch, and I anticipate I will take around twenty minutes to implement it. I intend to use magnetic boards as a story prop to make the story more interesting and accessible to all the chidren.

RATIONALE

A story session is a valuable activity because it allows children to learn new vocabulary and it fosters listening skills. It encourages concentration, extends the child's knowledge and understanding of the world, and aids imagination through the child's own interpretation and involvement in the story. 'Books and stories provide a foundation for future learning and can be used to gain information as well as giving children the chance to gain experience of events and places they would not otherwise come into contact with' (Class handout, 6/1/99).

Imaginary play allows children to experience the roles of others and encourages social interaction. They also learn to take turns and share equipment, as well as to express their feelings, both positive and negative. Imaginary play presents opportunities to participate in other cultures and encourages appreciation of other children's life experiences. 'The capacity to play imaginatively is related to such skills as problem solving, logical thinking, creativity and divergent thinking' (Class handout, 9/12/98).

Books are an ideal way of presenting positive world images to children. They give them the opportunity to develop respect for people from all sorts of back-grounds regardless of gender, race, culture, ability or disability. It is important that I offer all the activities available to all the children, avoid stereotyping and be a positive role model so that children do not develop limited expectations.

Before reading books to children I should check the illustrations for stereo-types. I should also make sure people with special needs are not depicted as being weak and needy. In the nursery setting there should be books in heritage languages so that bilingual children and their parents/carers feel valued and their language recognised as important. Dual language books improve the achievements of bilingual children as well as extending everyone's knowledge.

When I carry out my story session I am going to use laminated story props on a magnetic board. I feel that story props are a good method of varying the presenta-tion of stories. They also help to convey the meaning of the story and allow the children to be actively involved, especially bilingual children for whom peer group interaction is vitally important.

PROPOSED LEARNING OUTCOMES FOR THE CHILDREN

When implementing this activity I hope that the children will learn respect for the ideas of others when asking questions and discussing the story, and learn to share and take turns. I hope the story will also foster concentration and listening skills, extend the children's knowledge and understanding of the world, aid the development of imagination and stimulate imaginary play and extend their vocabulary and ideas. Story sessions 'allow children to identify closely with the people and situations in the story and give rise to a good deal of conversation' (Matterson, 1977).

Learning songs and rhymes can aid recall and memory; whilst the use of repeti-tive stories and rhymes will contribute to increased language skills in those chil-dren who are bilingual.

The children will recognise that pictures and words have meaning, and that pic-tures are a representation of reality. They will also learn that books are fun and can be a useful method of finding out information and something to be cherished and looked after. Stories also encourage early literacy skills by encouraging recogni-tion of text and directionality. Clear illustrations will extend the children's appreciations of beauty. Their powers of imagination are enhanced by recalling the past or looking forward to future events and by using language to create imaginary situations.

PROPOSED LEARNING OUTCOMES FOR THE CANDIDATE

I will learn to take the chidren's developmental age into account, as well as how much experience they've had of group story sessions. The appropriateness of the book also needs to be thought about. I will learn to read stories in a way which the children will enjoy. I will learn to take care in choosing books to avoid stereotyping in the areas of race, religion, class, age, disability or gender. Positive images reflecting the diversity of culture and families today, need to be included, together with stories portraying children with special needs and girls in strong roles. I will learn to be aware of the individual needs of the children in my group to ensure that the story sessions are of value to them and that they are gaining developmentally from them. 'Books and stories should be part of every child's experience and are valuable in developing knowledge attitudes and habits which will be useful at a later stage' (Matterson, 1977). I will learn which books best stimulate the imagination and lead to imaginary play.

REVIEW/EVALUATION

Prior to reading the story I distributed my story props amongst the children present. I read the story to 19 children and not 12 as originally planned. However, this increase in the number of listeners did not detract from the story, in fact it added to it. As the story progressed, the child with the prop would come up and stick it onto the magnetic board. The children all remained interested and maintained good concentration right until the end. I think this was due to being actively involved in the story (through the use of props) and also because of the repetitive language. For example, every time 'Claire' met a friend she would say the same thing to encourage them to ask how she hurt her knee. After a few pages my audience began to anticipate what 'Claire' would say and would all join in with me. They all displayed good observation skills and recognition of animals and objects, as although unable to read, they knew what animal or object was due to appear next. In fact the only interruptions occurred when the children were quizzing each other as to who had the next story prop in their possession. Whilst reading the story, I sometimes repeated a sentence or a noise, just to encourage more active participation from the children. They didn't let me down and responded magnificently each time.

I think that the children and I gained all the things I previously stated in the proposed learning outcomes. They took turns to ask questions when the story was finished and they showed respect for each other by listening. Their concentration and listening skills were definitely heightened, which was illustrated by their answers to my questions about the story when the session was over. Their imagination was aided through their involvement in the story. I learnt a great deal about planning and time from this story session. Without adequate thought, preparation and presentation, this story session would not have been successful. The children's attention and concentration would have waned because there would have been nothing to hold it, apart from my voice. I also learnt to relax and laugh whilst reading and this positive enjoyment of the story session seemed to have been communicated to my audience. The bilingual children in my class were certainly helped by the story props as this made the story come alive for them, and they were able to fully participate and feel included, not excluded. After the session some of the children pretended to be the animals in the story.

PLANS FOR THE FUTURE

My story session will involve the children making the story props themselves with some guidance. I will also tell the story without the book so as to maintain eye contact with my audience, which I feel is an important factor in their understanding of the story.

I will implement some linked activites from the story session to further enhance the experience.

BIBLIOGRAPHY

Donoghue T. (6/1/99) Class handout.
Donoghue T. (9/12/98) Class handout.
Hobart C. and Frankel J., 1995, *A Practical Guide to Activities for Young Children*, Stanley Thornes (Publishers) Ltd.
Hobart C. and Frankel J., 1996, *A Practical Guide to Working with Young Children*, 2nd edition, Stanley Thornes (Publishers) Ltd.
Matterson E.M., 1977, *Play with A Purpose For Under-Sevens*, Penguin Books.

Routines

A 'routine' is an activity that happens on a regular basis, either hourly, daily, weekly or even annually. To complete Unit 2, you will be asked to demonstrate your knowledge of a 24-hour routine for a baby under a year and to describe the daily routine within a placement setting that you have helped to implement. Unit 2 was devised by CACHE to help students reflect on and evaluate their practice. The following routine was devised by a DCE student in her second term.

The Certificate in Child Care and Education Course (CCE) requires you to do a number of planned activities, some of which are concerned with play and the provision of activities for children. The overview will describe in detail the particular activities. You may find the Evaluation of Activities sheet on page 145 useful.

ROUTINE

INTRODUCTION

This assignment focuses on my ability to design a routine for a three-year-old child who attends the morning sessions at a nursery class. This routine will be established from the moment the child awakes in the morning until the time he goes to bed in the evening.

AIM

The aim of this assignment is twofold: to establish a routine suitable for a three-year-old child and to ensure that the physical care, emotional, social and intellectual needs of the child are met and are achieved within a safe, secure, hazard-fee environment, where the child is able to play, discover, explore and learn without restriction.

RATIONALE

This rationale underlines the principles and importance of planning a routine for a young child. There are many advantages to routines, not just for the child but also for the primary carers, nursery staff and the wider society. Routines are important as they encourage, in children, a skill which is necessary for life. Teaching them from a young age heightens awareness and encourages independence and an understanding of the importance of carrying out specific tasks throughout their day, for example hand-washing. Routines give children a feeling of stability: knowing that some events throughout their day and week are predictable offers a child a sense of security and well-being. Children enjoy knowing, for example that they attend nursery on Monday morning.

Routines occur daily within nursery surroundings such as washing hands after going to the toilet, before and after mealtimes, after playing outside or with soil or sand, sneezing, coughing, after messy play, etc. This allows staff and educators not to have to continually tell children to go and wash their hands because when children adjust to this routine situation they will do it automatically. Although new children who participate will slowly learn to adjust to routines, some may not be taught a routine in family life. This can be achieved through nursery staff being positive role models and stressing the importance of routines. Hobart and Frankel (1996) claim that 'you should present yourself as a good role model and encourage the children to think about their health in a positive way'.

It is important that any routine must be designed to meet the physical, emotional, social and learning needs of the individual child. The routine has to be established within a safe and secure environment for the child, parent/carer and staff. Safety is the main priority as the welfare of the child is paramount. The environment has to be hazard-free, and equipment must be checked regularly, for example construction bricks as Hobart and Frankel (1995) claim that 'wooden blocks need to be checked regularly for splinters', and paint used must be non-toxic. The physical environment must be safe and equipment should be moved if necessary to increase the amount of space, allowing children ease of access so encouraging independence in exploration and enabling wheelchair access. Temperature and lighting should be adjusted to meet specific needs. The outside environment has to be safe so that children can release emotional frustration and aggression and develop their fine and gross motor skills. The ground has to be examined for dangerous objects, in particular glass which presents one of the biggest safety hazards to young children. Regularly monitoring equipment and ensuring the nursery staff establish a routine every morning, checking that equipment is safe, will ensure that children can play safely. The child's primary carer must maintain a safe home environment, e.g. ensuring toys have the Lion mark, that safety sockets are in a place that prevents investigation by small fingers, that circuit breakers are used, that matches are not left about the house, that bath water is at the correct temperature, that small children do not sleep on bunk beds as a small child may roll off and that children know the correct way of walking up the stairs.

The routine must demonstrate that the parent/carer is the main educator of the child as the parent/carer understands their child's needs, capabilities, diet and health better than anyone else. There must be good communication between the child, parent/carer and nursery staff in order to establish an effective partnership. According to Bruce (1997), 'the key to partnership with parents lies in having a network of strategies which can be employed so that different approaches are used with different families'. If an effective partnership is established then nursery staff and primary carers can build a close, open, confident relationship where they can exchange information about the physical, emotional, social and intellectual needs of the child. Together, the nursery staff and primary carers working as one can design a suitable routine which suits the needs of the child.

Throughout the day the routine must include one-to-one interaction between adult and child. This can take place during the morning with the nursery staff and later on with the main carer. One-to-one interaction is important for the child and the adult as it offers opportunities for both to form close relationships, allowing the nursery staff to focus on one particular child and that child's needs whether they are learning, social or emotional needs, and it allows the child to express him/herself openly. Whilst at home the parent/carer should try to maintain one-to-one interaction with her child to establish a positive relationship, offer the child security, and praise achievements in order to raise self-esteem and self-image.

Every family is different and has different needs so routines have to be made to suit the child's needs and made appropriate to fit in with the life style of the family. Different families have individual circumstances. Considering employment, for example, a single parent may require the routine to be made flexible to fit around his/her working schedule. If the parent/carer works in the morning then the routine may require that the child attends the morning session and remains for lunch or it may be arranged that a relative, friend or nanny collects the child. It may be the case that the child attends the afternoon sessions because the primary carer works then. According to Geraghty (1990), one-parent families are often allocated a full-time nursery placement. Routines also recognise that different families have different numbers of children who are at different ages and stages in their life and development and take this into consideration. For example a mother with a child who attends nursery and who also has a young baby needs to establish a routine that ensures the child is well cared for, is learning and exploring all the time, and that rest, socialisation and emotional needs are met but also to ensure that the routine fits around the baby's feeding time, nappy changing, health checks etc.

A child should have a routine to meet his/her needs and give stability in his/her life but which should be made flexible to account for changes, such as an outing to the library or to the local farm. According to Geraghty (1990) 'generally, the nursery should include a daily routine to provide predictability of events and security but also flexibility to allow for changes of timetable'. If changes do occur to a child in the routine at nursery or home, always provide the child with reassurance to give them security.

Every routine must include and promote physical care. The emotional, social and learning needs of the child have to be met. The routine has to recognise children who have special needs. The Warnock report provided the basis of the 1981 Education Act where it stated that children and young people disadvantaged by disabilities of mind and body should, where possible, be integrated into mainstream schools. Special educational needs were defined as mild, moderate or severe and assessments of a child's specific needs should be ongoing as should the statementing process which aims to identify the area of need and define the treatment/education requirements for such areas.

Within nurseries, equipment should be adjusted to meet all needs. Partially sighted children need play materials they can feel, magnifiers, talking books, large print, tape recorders and braille. Partially hearing children require visual interpretation of the spoken word, signs and pictures. There is specific need for exercise to help in children's emotional development to relieve aggression and frustration.

Exercise and outdoor play promotes good health, helps improve breathing and circulation and promotes resistence to infection. Exposure to fresh air and sunlight improves physical development as sunrays acting on the skin produce vitamin D.

Routines have to take into consideration cultural and religious needs, and these needs have to be respected. Routines must be designed to consider that different cultures and religions may require different diets.

Health is very important both when the child is at home and in the nursery setting. The health and safety policy must be observed so as to maintain good health
and safety. This policy must be regularly reviewed.

Within the routine, sleep and rest for the child is very important especially
after physical exercise/activity. According to Beaver et al. (1995), 'the benefits
of rest are:

- to allow tissues to recover
- the heart rate will fall
- to allow oxygen to be replaced
- for body temperature to drop.'

Sometimes, it is hard to get children to sleep for they may feel that they are
missing out on something important. Establishing a routine that involves rest/sleep
periods will encourage good habits so the child won't refuse resting periods.
Resting periods are also important for the primary carer and educator as they provide times to do things around the house that might be necessary. Beaver et al.
(1995) claims that 'using a familiar routine and reassurance that carers are nearby
may encourage children who are unwilling to go to bed to settle more willingly'.

When devising a child's routine there must be recognition of the curriculum so
that the key worker in the nursery setting can plan a range of different experi-
ences/activities that promotes the child's needs in all areas of development: physical, intellectual, social, emotional and linguistic. Very often these experiences
are based around a specific theme or topic that is developed over several sessions
that the child attends.

PROPOSED LEARNING OUTCOMES FOR THE CHILD

I want the child to learn the importance of establishing a routine, how and why it
is done, and the reasons why we as nursery staff and primary carers stress the
importance of attending to personal hygiene. I want the child to learn to accept
people and children from various cultures and religions or who have a special need,
etc, and help the child develop a positive attitude. The child should also learn
good social skills and this can be fully achieved by designing the routine to create learning experiences that encourage sharing, co-operation and offer the child
responsibility over his environment through looking after it. Making occasional
changes to the routine will help the child learn to be flexible.

I would like the child to learn:

- the importance of washing hands after specific events during the nursery session
  and at home to prevent the spread of infection
- the value of personal hygiene, regular exercise and rest
- good socialisation skills through sharing the play equipment, co-operating and
  developing good communications skills
- to adjust to a suitable routine that is flexible
- a sense of responsibility through growing independence
- to have control over his emotional feelings, for example: anger.
- to feel safe and secure when placed in two different environments: home setting
  and nursery surroundings
- to understand the value of brushing teeth three times a day and that caring for
  teeth helps prevent decay, gives healthy gums, etc.
- the value of outside play in the nursery playground and perhaps in the garden
  provided at home. This will help to teach the child delight and respect for the
  natural world and help to promote knowledge and understanding of the world
- the value of all types of play within the child's day
- to use spoken language correctly, to be able to expand vocabulary, and value
  communication between children and adults
- understand the need for rest and sleep periods to be implemented within the
  child's daily routine
- through a wide range of experiences and activities.

PROPOSED LEARNING OUTCOMES FOR THE CANDIDATE

I want to develop an understanding of safety awareness, participate more within the
child's nursery establishment, connect and have good communication with colleagues,
prepare the child for any changes within the routine and be a positive role model
for the child.

I would like to learn:
- to develop my awareness of children's safety, as the welfare of the child is paramount
- to provide a good physical environment in order to increase the child's independence, physical security and self-confidence
- to present myself as a positive role model to the child
- to establish a routine that is suitable for all the needs of the child
- to prepare the child for any changes that may occur within his daily routine
- to establish a good effective partnership with the team of the nursery
- how the child reacts to different situations as they arise, for example, if the child went to bed at a different time, whether he would wake up feeling refreshed or still tired
- about the way in which the child acts socially in the nursery, whether he shares, co-operates and communicates well, using spoken language
- about the range of activities that the child does in nursery so that I can implement them at home and at the same time provide a suitable environment.

THE ROUTINE

TIME	ACTIVITY
7:45	Child wakes up
8:00	Child gets washed, brushes teeth, puts clean clothes on
8:30	Child has breakfast: cereal, 1 glass of milk
8:55	Depart for nursery – walking
9:15	Arrive at nursery
9:30	Free class activities
10:00	Child goes to music room with class
10:20	Child outside in playground
11:00	Snack time: milk and 2 biscuits
11:15	Child doing a painting and tidy-up-time
11:30	Child sitting down on carpet listening to story, singing nursery rhymes
11:50	Child collected from nursery
12:15	Arrive home: child washes hands, has lunch: chicken nuggets, green vegetables, brown bread, 1 glass of water and an apple
12:45	Walk to the park. Child plays on swings, roundabout, slide, climbing frame, kicks a football about with primary carer
1:30	Arrive home, washes hands. Child has a sleep with his favourite comforter (teddy)
2:30	Child outside in the garden
3:00	Washes hands. Child and carer go shopping
3:50	Arrive home, washes hands. Child has a snack: 1 glass of milk and a banana
4:10	Child and carer take part in a creative activity. Washes hands
4:30	Child has a small rest period, watching TV
5:00	Child washes hands. Child has main meal: fish, mashed potato, carrots, peas, 1 glass of water, jelly and ice cream
5:30	Storytime
6:00	Child has bath
6:20	Child puts night clothes on
6:30	Child brushes teeth
6:40	Child gets into bed along with his favourite comforter. We sing nursery rhymes that he learnt in nursery that morning
7:00	Child falls asleep

EVALUATION

Physical care

Within my routine I emphasise the importance of washing hands. Geraghty (1990) claims that 'hands are a potent source of infection and need to be washed more frequently than the rest of the body especially after going to the toilet and before preparation, serving and eating of food'. Stressing the importance of healthy hygiene teaches a child healthy habits for life, encouraging independence and increasing self-confidence. In my routine, hand washing is mentioned several times to stress the importance of it.

The benefits of having a bath time every evening within the daily routine are that it is a time where the child can relax, it's necessary for the removal of dirt and micro-organisms, and it allows the child the freedom to play and explore with a range of bath toys in water play. The primary carer's role is to supervise bath time at all times because it has been known for children to drown in only a few inches of water. Ensure that the water temperature is just right for the child because if it is too hot the child can burn himself. With water that is too hot or too cold the child may come to dislike bath time. I must ensure that the child doesn't stand, as injuries may arise if he falls. I will use a non-slip mat. According to Beaver et al. (1995), 'this routine care includes frequent observation of the condition of the skin for any rashes or areas of soreness.'

Also in the routine the child has access to frequent outdoor play both at the nursery and at home. This helps the child's development of fine and gross motor skills, releases surplus energy, stimulates the appetite, aids digestion, helps improve circulation and breathing, promotes sleep, gives resistance to infection and a healthy skin and helps to produce vitamin D for the child.

Within my routine, the child has two main meals during the day and two snacks. The aim is to provide the child with the correct nutritional requirements, which include carbohydrates, fats, protein, vitamins, minerals and water.

Sleep is stressed throughout the daily routine because this plays an important part in teaching the child the value of sleep and rest periods. Sleep offers the opportunity for the muscles and the body's metabolic processes to recover, and during sleep, a growth hormone is released to renew tissue and produce new bone and red blood cells.

Emotional needs

Outdoor play both in nursery and at home enables the child to release tension, frustration and aggression. Allowing the child to have a comforter when he is going to sleep or having rest periods will make him feel more secure and safe.

The primary carer's role is to always reassure the child that she is nearby and to establish a safe environment when the child is playing outside as injuries can occur with dangerous objects e.g. glass.

Raising self-esteem can be achieved through nursery care staff and primary educator praising a child's achievements. Children with disabilities require a lot of self-confidence and a good self-image in order for them to feel safe and secure within their environment.

Social needs

Within this daily routine there are many opportunities for the child to engage in socialisation both in his nursery routine and when he visits the park in the afternoon with his primary carer. Socialising teaches the child sharing skills, good communication through speech and co-operation with others. When the child is in the nursery he is able to mix with children of his own age. He is able to share and collaborate and gain responsibility of sharing space. He is also gaining confidence in being able to go up to other children with whom he is not familiar. The primary carer's role is to ensure that the child behaves in a way that is socially acceptable to others. The primary carer must encourage good play activities and encourage sharing.

Learning needs

Learning needs are based on a child's intellectual ability and what activities/experiences are enjoyed. This is the basis on which childcare workers establish the curriculum. Learning opportunities take place in the nursery and at home. Within his nursery setting the child is learning about the natural world outside in the playground, and at home in the garden. He is gaining a knowledge and understanding of his world and can explore throughout his daily routine.

The child's learning needs are also being met through the opportunity he has to listen to stories both in nursery and before he goes to bed at night. Saying nursery rhymes and singing enables the child to expand his vocabulary and fosters imagination and encourages a delight in language.

Learning needs at home and in nursery must allow for the child to explore and discover. One-to-one attention with the primary educator and sharing what the child is being taught at nursery enables child and parent/carer to continue to establish a close relationship.

BIBLIOGRAPHY

Beaver M., Brewster J., Jones P., Keene A., Neaum S. and Tallack J., 1995, *Babies and Young Children: Book 2* (ch. 13, p. 195), Stanley Thornes (Publishers) Ltd.
Bruce, T., 1997, *Early Childhood Education* (ch. 9, p. 151), Hodder & Stoughton.
Geraghty P., 1990, *Caring for Children* (ch. 1, p. 16; ch. 4, p. 109), Baillière Tindell.
Hobart C. and Frankel J., 1996, *A Practical Guide to Working With Young Children* 2nd edition, Stanley Thornes (Publishers) Ltd.
Hobart C. and Frankel J., 1995, *A Practical Guide to Activities For Young Children*, Stanley Thornes (Publishers) Ltd.

Portfolios

Unit 2 of the DCE requires you to compile a portfolio of your curriculum plans, detailed activity plans, resources and routines. It must include a table of contents, and contain a statement declaring the authenticity of the work.

The CCE requires you to keep a portfolio of all your work undertaken in the placement. It will include diaries, logs, observations, additional activities you have carried out with the children, and examples of leaflets and records from the placement. Your portfolio activities will be included, as well as references and a bibliography.

Your placement supervisor must sign all pieces of work. Confidentiality must be maintained at all times, and parental permission obtained in writing for any material that might identify the child or the family. It is your responsibility to make sure that your portfolio is kept in a safe place. Obtain a receipt if you hand it over to your tutor or supervisor.

You may, as an NVQ candidate, be asked to compile a portfolio of a range of activities that you have carried out with children.

The following checklists will help you ensure that your assignments have covered all the essential areas.

Practical considerations

- Discuss your proposed activity with your assessor or line manager. Make sure your establishment has the resources and materials you need, considering the cost within the total budget.
- What safety and equal opportunity issues are relevant to this activity?
- Ensure that the activity is age appropriate.
- Plan the timing: decide how long it will take and agree with other staff when you are going to carry out this activity
- Remember to protect the area, if necessary, and the children's clothing.

Value of the activity to the children

- What areas of development will this activity extend and promote?
- How can the children be involved in the planning, setting up and clearing away of the activity?
- How does this activity link in with a current theme or project, or the early years goals of the National Curriculum?
- What opportunities are there to enhance communication and build relationships?

Evaluating the activity

- Talk about how it went with the children and with your assessor or line manager.
- Had you planned adequately?
- Did you feel the children were fully involved?
- Did you think it went well?

- How could you improve it next time?
- What were the benefits for the children and for the establishment?

Complete the evaluation forms on pages 145 and 146.

The more activities you plan and prepare, the more skilled and competent you will become. As you evaluate your planning and the implementation of your activities, you will become a professional and reflective practitioner.

Appendices

Activities for children 5 to 7 years

LANGUAGE IN THE NATIONAL CURRICULUM

Proposed Activity: _____

Describe how some of the concepts below may be developed or encouraged during the activity.

Listening:	Stories	
	Music	
	Conversation	
Talking:	Discussion	
	Conversation	
Writing:	Early pre-writing	
	Writing	
Reading:	Pre-reading	
	Handling books	
	Reading	

Activities for children 5 to 7 years

MATHEMATICS IN THE NATIONAL CURRICULUM

Proposed Activity: _____

Describe how some of the concepts below may be developed or encouraged during the activity.

Conservation	
One-to-one correspondence	
Sequencing and counting	
Shapes	
Sorting	
Spatial relationships	
Time	
Symbols	
Patterns	
Money	
Estimating and measuring:	
Weight	
Height	
Width	
Volume	
Capacity	
Quantity	
Mathematical language	

Activities for children 5 to 7 years

SCIENCE IN THE NATIONAL CURRICULUM

Proposed Activity: _____

Describe how some of the concepts below may be developed or encouraged during the activity.

Exploring	
Using the five senses	
Gathering information	
Discovery	
Sorting and classifying	
Recording	
Experimenting	
Making changes	
Predicting and making hypothesis	
Scientific language	

Activities for children 1 to 7 years

EVALUATION OF ACTIVITIES

Activity: _____

What went well?
What went wrong?
Did you meet all the aims of the activity?
Did the activity allow active collaboration and involvement of the children?
What would you change in future plans?
How would you follow up this activity?
How does it link to future activities?
For infant school activities: how did you involve the children in the learning process?

Activities for children 1 to 7 years

MONITORING FOR EQUAL OPPORTUNITIES

Activity: _____

How does the activity encourage collaborative learning at some point in the process?
List the opportunities for the development of language.
How does the structure of the activity provide access for all the children?
How could the activity recognise the validity of all the children's cultures and backgrounds?
How does the activity encourage children to develop social and interpersonal skills:

Matrix to show links between activities and NVQ Child Care and Education Units

Level 2

	Natural materials	Cooking	Imaginary play	Painting and drawing	Creative art activities	Small and large construction	Puzzles and table-top games	Books and storytelling	Music and movement	Outside play	Outings	Festivals	Display and interest tables	Information technology
C1.3 Support opportunities for children's exercise	•		•	•					•	•	•			
C4.4 Help children to recognise and deal with their feelings	•	•	•	•	•	•		•	•				•	
C8.1 Provide activities, equipment and materials for creative play	•	•	•				•	•	•					•
C8.2 Play games with children			•				•	•	•	•				•
C8.3 Assist with cooking activities	•	•										•		
C8.4 Provide opportunities and equipment for manipulative play	•			•	•	•	•		•		•	•	•	•
C8.5 Examine objects of interest with children													•	
C9.4 Select and display books								•	•				•	
C9.5 Relate stories and rhymes								•				•	•	
E1.2 Prepare and maintain displays						•								
E2.6 Maintain the safety of children on outings										•	•			
C13.3 Encourage development through stimulation (babies)	•		•	•	•	•	•	•	•	•	•			
M1.1 Prepare equipment	•		•	•	•	•	•	•	•	•			•	•
M1.2 Prepare materials	•		•	•	•	•	•	•	•		•	•	•	•
M1.3 Monitor and store materials	•	•	•	•	•	•		•	•	•		•	•	•
P9.3 Encourage parents to participate in children's activities			•					•	•		•	•	•	•

Matrix to show links between activities and NVQ Child Care and Education Units *continued*

Level 3

	Natural materials	Cooking	Imaginary play	Painting and drawing	Creative art activities	Small and large construction	Puzzles and table-top games	Books and storytelling	Music and movement	Outside play	Outings	Festivals	Display and interest tables	Information technology
C3.1 Develop children's confidence in movement	•								•	•				
C3.2 Develop children's skills of locomotion and balance	•								•	•				
C3.3 Develop children's gross motor skills	•	•		•					•	•	•			
C3.4 Develop children's fine motor skills		•	•	•		•			•					•
C5.2 Enable children to relate to others	•	•	•	•	•	•	•	•	•	•	•	•		
C5.3 Develop children's self-reliance and self-esteem			•	•	•	•	•	•	•	•	•	•		•
C5.4 Enable children to recognise and deal with their feelings			•	•	•	•	•		•					
C5.5 Enable children to develop a positive self image and identity			•	•	•							•	•	•
C10.1 Develop children's attention span and memory		•				•	•		•				•	
C10.2 Develop children's awareness and understanding of sensory experiences	•	•	•		•				•			•		
C10.3 Develop children's understanding of mathematics and science	•	•				•	•		•	•	•	•	•	•
C10.4 Develop children's imagination and creativity	•	•	•			•		•	•				•	
C11.2 Provide activities, equipment and materials to extend and reinforce children's language and communication development	•	•	•	•	•	•		•		•	•	•	•	•
C11.3 Share books, stories and rhymes to expand children's language and communication development								•	•					•
C11.4 Provide communication opportunities to enhance and reinforce children's language and communication	•	•				•	•		•	•	•	•	•	•

Matrix to show links between activities and NVQ Child Care and Education Units *continued*

Level 3 *continued*

	Natural materials	Cooking	Imaginary play	Painting and drawing	Creative art activities	Small and large construction	Puzzles and table-top games	Books and storytelling	Music and movement	Outside play	Outings	Festivals	Display and interest tables	Information technology
P5.3 Provide feedback to parents about their involvement in children's activities	•	•	•	•	•	•	•	•	•	•	•	•	•	•
C14.4 Provide stimulation to foster the development of babies	•		•			•	•	•	•	•	•			
C14.5 Promote the language development of babies	•		•		•			•	•					
C17.1 Enable children with special needs to participate in activities	•	•	•	•	•	•	•	•	•	•	•	•	•	•
C17.5 Contribute to the inclusion of children with special needs	•	•	•	•	•	•	•	•	•	•	•	•	•	•
C24.1 Help develop chidren's reading skills		•	•					•			•	•	•	•
C24.2 Help develop children's comprehension skills	•	•	•				•	•			•	•	•	•
C24.3 Help develop children's writing skills	•		•	•	•									•
C25.1 Help children to use and apply mathematics	•	•	•	•	•	•	•		•	•	•		•	•
C25.2 Support children's understanding and use of number	•	•	•	•	•	•	•		•	•	•		•	•
C25.3 Help children develop their understanding and use of shape, space and measure	•		•			•	•						•	•
M7.2 Develop individual learning programmes for children	•	•	•	•	•	•	•	•	•	•	•	•	•	•
M7.3 Implement planned learning activities	•	•	•	•	•	•	•	•	•	•	•	•	•	•
M7.4 Evaluate planned learning activities and experiences	•	•	•	•	•	•	•	•	•	•	•	•	•	•
M7.11 Plan a curriculum to facilitate children's learning and development	•	•	•	•	•	•	•	•	•	•	•	•	•	•

General Resources

Books

BAECE, *Play: the Key to Young Children's Learning*, from BAECE (for address see Organisations, page 152)

Brown B., 1993, *All Our Children*, BBC Educational Publishing.

Bruce T., 1996, *Helping Young Children to Play*, Hodder & Stoughton.

Cash T., 1989, *Science is Child's Play*, Longman.

Clemson W. and D., 1994, Action Maths Series, Two-Can Publishing.

Curtis A., 1986, *A Curriculum for the Pre-school Child*, NFER Nelson.

Derman-Sparks L., 1989, *Anti-Bias Curriculum*, National Association for the Education of Young Children, Washington DC.

Dixon B., 1990, *Playing Them False*; 1977, *Catching Them Young*, Trentham Books.

Early Childhood Education Centre, *Fun Together*, from Stand House School, Queen Mary Road, Sheffield S2 1HX.

Early Years Curriculum Group, 1989, *Early Childhood Education*, Trentham Books.

Einon D., 1985, *Creative Play*, Penguin.

Fountain S., 1990, *Learning Together – Cooperative Games and Activities*, Centre for Global Education.

Garvey C., 1991, *Play* (2nd Edition), Developing Child Series, Fontana.

Goldschmied E. and Jackson S., 1994, *People Under Three*, Routledge.

Hall N. and Abbot L. (Eds), 1994, *Play in the Primary Curriculum*, Hodder & Stoughton Ltd.

Jameson K. and Kidd P., 1986, *Pre-School Play*, Unwin Paperbacks.

Leer R., 1990, *Play Helps* (3rd Edition), 1993 and *More Play Helps*, Heinemann.

Maidenhead Teachers Centre, 1982, *Doing Things In and About the Home*, Trentham Books.

Matterson E., 1965, *Play with a Purpose for Under Sevens*, Penguin Books.

Matusiak C., 1990, *Maths Activities*, Bright Ideas for Early Years Series, Scholastic Publications Ltd.

Miller N., 1967, *Children's Games from Many Lands*, Friendship Press, New York.

Morris J. and Mort L., 1990, *Learning Through Play* and *Getting Started*, Bright Ideas for Early Years, Scholastic Publications Ltd.

PPA, 1991, *Equal Chances*, PPA Series.

PPA, *Building for the Future: equal opportunities for under fives through play in groups*, PPA, Wiltshire.

PPA, *Play and Learning for Under Threes*, from PPA Promotion, 45–49 Union Road, Croydon CRO 2XU.

Rappaport L. et al., *Play and Learning for All Children – Creative play activities for children with disabilities*, Human Kinetics.

Sheridan M.D., 1985, *Spontaneous Play in Early Childhood*, NFER.
Mango Spice – 44 Caribbean Songs, 1981, A. & C. Black (Publishers) Ltd.

Series

Blueprint Series is an expanding series of practical ideas and photocopiable resources for use in primary schools, published by Stanley Thornes (Publishers) Ltd.

Bright Ideas for Early Years Series, Bright Ideas Series, Learning Through Play Series and Themes for Early Years Series are published by Scholastic Publications Ltd, Freepost, CV1034, Westfield Road, Southam, Leamington Spa, Warwicks CV33 0BR.

Nottingham Educational Supplies, Ludlow Hill Road, West Bridgeforth, Nottingham NG2 6HD, publish several Pre-school Activities booklets including *Get Moving* NB 3369/5; *Multicultural Play* NB 3370/5; *Imaginative Play* NB 3371/8.

Toy Libraries Association (for address see Organisations, page 152) with the British Toy and Hobby Association (for address see Lion Mark, page 152) publish Playmatters, practical books for young children: *The Good Toy Guide*, *Talk To Me*, *Do It Yourself*, *Mucky Play*, *Hear and Say*, *Look and Touch*, *Ready to Play* (9 booklets), *Positions for Play*, *Toy Care*, *I Can Use My Hands*, and *Toys and Play in Child Development*.

Videos

Albany Video, *Being White* and *Coffee Coloured Children*, from Albany Video Distribution, Battersea Studios, Television Centre, Thackeray Road, London SW8 3TW.

BAECE, *Our Present is Our Future*, from BAECE (for address see Organisations, page 152).

Community Playthings, *Equipped to Play*, from Community Playthings (for address see Catalogues and Equipment).

Moonlight films, *Marked for Life*, Mosaic Series, BBC, for information write to BBC Education, 201 Wood Lane, London W12 7TS. Telephone 0181 752 5252.

Catalogues and equipment

Criteria for Play Equipment, Community Playthings, Robertsbridge, East Sussex TN32 5DR. Telephone Freephone 0800 387 457. Also available free on request from Community Playthings is a full colour catalogue of special furniture and equipment for children with disabilities.

Galt Toys, Brookfield Road, Cheadle, Cheshire SK8 2PN. Telephone 0161 4289111.

Hope Pre-School Catalogue, Orb Mill, Huddersfield Road, Oldham, Lancs OL4 2ST.

NES Arnold, Ludlow Hill Road, West Bridgford, Nottingham NG 6HD. Telephone 01602 452201.

Rompa, Goyt Side Road, Chesterfield, Derbyshire S40 2PH. Telephone 0645 211777. (Products for children with hearing disabilities.)

Organisations

British Association for Early Childhood Education (BAECE), 111 City View House, 463 Bethnal Green Road, London E2 9QH.

Early Years Trainers Anti-Racist Network (EYTARN), PO Box 1870, London N12 8JQ.

Disabled Living Foundation, 380/384 Harrow Road, London W9 2HU. Telephone 0171 289 6111.

MAPA – Play for Disabled Children, Fulham Palace, Bishops Avenue, London SW6 6EA. Telephone 0171 731 1435.

National Children's Bureau, 8 Wakley Street, London EC1V 7QE.

National Early Years Network (until recently, VOLCUF), 77 Holloway Road, London N7 81Z. Telephone 0171 607 9573.

National Play Information Centre, 359/362 Euston Road, London NW1 3AL. Telephone 0171 3835455. Open 10–4 Monday to Friday.

National Playbus Association, Unit G, Amos Castle Estate, Junction Road, Brislington, Bristol BS4 5AJ. Telephone 0272 7753 75.

Pre-School Learning Alliance (formerly Pre-School Playgroups Association (PPA)), 61/63 Kings Cross Road, London WC1X 9LL.

Save the Children, Equality Learning Centre, The Resource Centre, 356 Holloway Road, London N7 6PA. Telephone 0171 700 8127.

Toy Libraries Association, 68 Churchway, London NW1 1LT.

Working Group Against Racism in Children's Resources, 460 Wandsworth Road, London SW8 3LX.

World Organization for Early Childhood Education (OMEP), c/o Thomas Coram Foundation, 40 Brunswick Square, London WC1N 1AU.

Education departments

In London: Museum of Mankind, The Commonwealth Institute, Science Museum, Natural History Museum, Bethnal Green Museum of Childhood etc.

Place to visit

Aklowa: an African traditional heritage village, offering many activities. For more information write to Aklowa, Takeley House, Brewer's End, Bishops Stortford, Herts CM22 6QR. Telephone 01279 871062.

Lion mark

BSS 5665/EN71, the toy industry symbol for safety and quality, was introduced in 1989. For more details write to The British Toy and Hobby Association, 80 Camberwell Road, London SE5 0EG. Telephone 0171 701 7271.